The Skeptical Buddha, The Tao of Science

To Serra

Who has been with me nearly every step of the way on my journey

into understanding the methodologies of both Science and Skepticism

and calling me out anytime I had way more certainty than the

evidence could support.

The Skeptical Buddha, The Tao of Science

Print version ISBN: 9798783520952
No ISBN for digital copy
Imprint: Independently published

Cover design and photo curation design by: Adam Collier
Edited By HR Croissant
Special Thanks to Desmond Wood for fact checking

Contents

Introduction

In my late twenties, as I was finding myself as a person, I would go into Borders or Barnes and Noble and pick up any number of reduced priced books. There I discovered eastern philosophy and dove headlong into Tai Chi, Feng Shui, Traditional Chinese Medicine and spent several thousand dollars of my student loans on acupuncture and chiropractic, believing I needed them to be healthy and that I was investing in my future.

I picked up a coffee table book of the Tao Te Ching, a beautifully illustrated hardback book and just devoured the philosophy. The Tao of Pooh and the Te of Piglet by Benjamin Hoff brought great calm and comfort to me (Hoff 2019). But my favorite book of all was a coffee table book with gorgeous photos by an author I will simply call "The Guru" for legal reasons, who discussed both Buddhism and Taoism. This impacted much of the rest of my early adult life.

In my early thirties, I was a vocal atheist and paired it with my eastern mysticism studies, and I began to think of them as complementary to each other. I still hold that this idea is true, depending on which branch and sub-branch of this mysticism you follow. However, as I began digging into the scientific and skeptical communities of the internet, before the term was summarily hijacked by the Alt-Right, I began to better understand skepticism as a practice and a journey. Never a destination. Similar to Buddhist enlightenment or awakening, my world view began to shift. I began finding scientific flaws in Feng Shui and Traditional Chinese Medicine, which curbed much of my beliefs to what I could deem scientifically validated.

A few years ago, I went back and read the old book by "The Guru" and began spotting flaws in it as well, mostly because I had a better understanding of science, history, nature and naturally evolved cognitive biases. I also, in passing, discovered that The Guru was what some would refer to as a cult leader who lived in the lap of luxury like so many Indian

Hindu gurus, similar to the ones the Beatles encountered. The Guru's top leadership was convicted of terrorism, but how much of his involvement is unknowable. He rebranded

Prior to around the 1960's, Buddhism and Taoism as explained by The Guru were mostly valid with what we knew about the human brain and science at the time, though lacking in nuance. Personally, without further study, I would have stayed knee-deep in the philosophy of this beautiful coffee table book without the knowledge learned of who was teaching it and who was shaping it. Sometimes a book serves better as a statement piece in a room than it does the brickwork for personal philosophy.

I will say, upon further reflection of The Guru, you can start to see how he aimed his message towards the rich, elite, and at the very least middle-class with disposable income. He touts materialism and ambition as a bad thing while using gifted items from his wealthy donors to have a proxy lavish lifestyle. He isolated himself from those who were starving while turning platitudes to rationalize his greed. His books are for the privileged, not the impoverished, because the poor cannot pay homage without money and the rich have more than they know what to do with, so he helped unburden them of that excess. In the modern era, we have developed newer and better ways to discover reality.

Prior to the 1960's, meditation, experience, and philosophical theory using logic were some of the ways to find self-truth. The problem being is that with so many varying subjective experiences and then the introduction of new mind altering drugs, many branches of mystic thought coupled with scam artists became more prevalent. Many of those ideologies that sprang up from that era still persist today, influencing people on how the mind works.

We have since discovered new criteria that narrows assumptions one can make about themselves and reality, allowing a straighter and more precise path to understanding oneself and others. This prevents just going with what you feel, which created a way of thinking that currently has a misnomer of postmodernism. Postmodernism, or more specifically the academic branch of it, Post-structuralism, was a skeptical critique of the modernist movement, which ignored the human element in study in favor of meta-narratives or collections of objective facts woven together in a narrative in a way that might not be correct, and without regard especially of those outside the white male colonialist experience and hegemony that held academia in an iron grip. However some people took this to an extreme and believed and propagated the idea that everyone's beliefs were equally valid. Post-structuralism was replaced a decade later with more pragmatic ideas but was at the time a necessary stepping-stone to better understand the world.

Prior to the 60's, Buddhism and Taoism as well as many other applied philosophies appeared to all be valid, but as we began discovering that the mind in some cases works counter-intuitively to how we assume it works, cracks began to form in many of the philosophies that had stood the test of time for millennia. But at the same time, science has backed up many parts of philosophies and practices to have real merit and we should all embrace those discoveries and ways of thinking.

Humans are visually and emotionally driven and there is the aesthetic angle to The Guru's book that drew me in and immersed me in my experience and calming effects. So I decided that there is no reason to throw the baby out with the bathwater; I can use this psychologically proven method to help in teaching as it generates what most religions classify as spiritual feelings, but I prefer the term from Japanese philosophical aesthetics called Yugen, which roughly translates to, "An awareness of the universe that triggers emotional responses too deep and mysterious for words." I will discuss this further near the end of the book.

And just one last thing, I have stories written in here, but they are amended and transliterated, with some artistic license. Part of this is because there are many versions of the same story, and there is an attempt to fuse them, and another is an attempt to translate the message better when some of the older translation and language isn't exactly useful in the modern era. So enjoy the story but realize that unlike what The Guru failed to tell me, this isn't the only or even the definitive version of the story. There are many. So if you want to know more, go to the original sources or sutras to discover them for yourself.

So, join me in a journey exploring eastern philosophy and thought and discover how they have helped to birth science, ethics and skepticism. We will dive into how these ideologies have changed and demonstrate when and how they were proven wrong with modern science. And there are pretty pictures along the way.

"If scientific analysis were conclusively to demonstrate certain claims in Buddhism to be false, then we must accept the findings of science and abandon those claims." - The 14th Dali Lama

Eastern Philosophy and Science

"The Tao that can be told is not the universal Tao. The name that cannot be named is not the universal name." The first lines from the Tao Te Ching. Potentially deep and meaningful words, perhaps missing translational nuance due to the two and a half thousand year changes that occur during the evolution of language or perhaps they are just rough ideas attempting to convey an idea that society had not yet invented.

"Truth one: Reality is Suffering." The first of the four Noble truths of Gautama Siddartha, also known as the Buddha. Suffering. A word with more nuance in the pali language, meaning not only pain and physical suffering but also emotional suffering such as disappointment. Even hearing the alarm clock in the morning brings a small amount of emotional suffering. His remedy for disappointment? Giving up attachment.

These two philosophies from the East have been much embraced by peoples of the West. They are referred to as religions, due to their sometimes-supernatural ties, or as philosophies because of their core principles of thought and questioning. They idealize doubt, contemplation and observation.

Skepticism is the ability to look at truth, not at what you would like it to be, or passionately believe it is, but look at the raw, boring and many times uncomforting data and see reality for what it actually is. All the while exhaustively thinking of every way one's own conclusions could be wrong, skewed or biased and listening to the people who may know details and nuances of those possible methods of bias and error. Buddhism is extremely heavy on seeking truth and focusing on what is real and getting one's own ego out of the way to embrace and face head on these discomforting truths of reality,

Science is a methodology used for analyzing reality. It involves using skepticism to ask nature questions and ensures you are not tricking yourself with your own bias. It relies on observing and collecting data, sometimes from comparing what we find occurred in the past with current findings such as geology or archeology, and many times by running long boring experiments over and over again and making observations and only making a decision about the reality of the experiment after all the data is in. Taoism is a philosophy that demands calm observation. It also focuses on looking at the whole instead of just looking at the sum of the parts. It works to eliminate distractions and appreciate not only what is solid and mass, but also the usefulness of what is not there, such as the empty space that makes up the interior of a house or a jar.

All philosophies including these two hold extremely powerful truths. Early philosophy had some things right and a lot of things wrong. Thanks to very cheap paper and the movable type printing press in Europe, however, books began to flow freely and cheaply in the West and people of all walks of life began to run into very beautifully sounding ideas that were all logically sound and complex but went completely counter to each other.

With the spread of knowledge through these texts, people were able to test philosophical ideas with their own observations and were able to decide for themselves which philosophical theories held up to scrutiny, and which of them just sounded "nice" and "logical." The concept of science was born as a methodology to test and disprove ideas. Over time, there was an explosion of discovery which led to new technology which led to more discovery, much like a lens getting further polished to make the blurry image more and more clear.

We now know so much more than we ever knew, especially about the brain and psychology. We are discovering things that both confirm what we thought we knew about the brain and things that are actually counter intuitive about our own minds. Discovering the parts of philosophies that are replicable by science, and discarding the parts that do not will be the only way to move us forward as human beings into the future.

The Skeptical
Buddha

Introduction to Buddhism

There are many legends surrounding the Man, Gautama Siddhartha. Quite a large number of stories mixed with myth or metaphor. Oral traditions ensured that stories would get bigger and more elaborate with each telling, as storytelling was the first infotainment. It is how our brains are wired to take in information best. It is why ancient stories are good at teaching lessons, but we should be extremely skeptical of the stories' historical fact. Thanks to our modern black and white distinctions between fiction and nonfiction, there are many metaphors in ancient stories that we miss. They are either true or false in our literal book-filled minds.

This "Tall Tale Used For Moral Lessons" narrative was even used in early colonial America where writers would use the founders as these mythical figureheads to pass on an ideology, such as with George Washington and the infamous Cherry Tree. After the civil war and modernism set in, we began to view things as distinctly fact or fiction and many teachers assumed that because there was a book about a historical figure, then it must be historically accurate. The past is a foreign country and these teachers who taught their classes the "truth" about these historical figures, had a serious translation problem. Most of early American "history" is post-hoc mythology. People would have understood this at the time in the same vein as oral tradition storytelling. However, modernity changed our understanding of categorization systems to better take in knowledge our ancestors could never consider without the printing press. Unfortunately this transition led to a translation error in how we assumed they viewed fact and fiction.

It is said that the Buddha was born, found enlightenment, and died on the exact same day of the year, in a holiday now commemorated in certain parts of southeast Asia called Vesak. Vesak is celebrated in the spring, and changes depending on the lunar calendar similar to Easter. This claim about his birth, enlightenment and death changes depending on the country and region. In some stories, his mother died upon his birth, or 7 days later. In some she became the very first Buddhist Nun, showing equality between the sexes in

Buddhism. In some stories it was his aunt instead who filled that role. In some he even emerged from his mother's armpit, a sign of purity as opposed to the "usual" impure route of birth. Some stories state he was already able to walk and talk upon his birth. His narrative changes for the needs of the area and with each grand retelling, a cultural telephone game of a legend. The different schools of thought came from legends of Buddha's 32 disciples, each of them starting their own schools of thought, branching out further and further as the philosophy spread out of India.

Buddhism began in northern India near Nepal. From there it branched out into many Asian nations, often fusing into the other native religions. Bon in Tibet, Traditional Taoist religion in China, Shinto in Japan. The Theravada branch is the oldest surviving branch of the various now extinct sects of Buddhism and claims to follow the "teachings of the elders," the literal translation of the word theravada. According to legend, 30 years after the death of the Buddha, a council was formed to record and preserve the teachings of the Buddha directly from his disciples. Their holy text is referred to as the Pali canon, as the oldest surviving copies are in the Pali language, which was a scholarly version of the regional vernacular the Buddha and his followers spoke called Prakrit. Pali had the same use as Latin eventually did in Christianity.

The Theravada branch is called the "little boat," which in southern Asia emphasized more on one's self getting closer to Nirvana. In some areas, Theravaden monks believed that locking themselves away in monasteries and keeping themselves from the common people was the way for enlightenment.

The Mahayana branch, called the "big boat," which started in southeast India but then became predominant in the rest of northern Asia and China, instead emphasized compassion and the parts of Buddhism that claimed one could find enlightenment by helping others find enlightenment. Some have taken this so far as to believe their job is to bring every single sentient being to enlightenment. In some branches, one could attain enlightenment just from reading the sutras or Buddhist holy texts. They also promoted the ideas of Bodhisattvas or other enlightened Buddhists similar to canonized saints that people can pray to and emulate. The Ch'an in China or Zen in Japan believed that the sutras are not as useful compared with thoughtful interaction with the world and shun the idea of concepts. They believe that one can receive instantaneous enlightenment in a flash of epiphany after enough practice of meditation and observation of oneself or nature and reality which occurs when the mind becomes unified. They not only follow the Pali canon, though translated into Chinese, but also their own extra tests.

One branch of Mahayana branched off taking in parts Hindu mysticism, called Mantrayana or Tantrayana, and used complex rituals and repetitions as a quicker way to enlightenment. It is referred to as tantric Buddhism, a complex concept we will discuss later. They use the Chinese canon as well as their own extra sutras (Harvey, 2015).

Let's just say that what the Buddha actually said and believed is very muddled and lost to history. He never actually wrote anything; his disciples wrote their interpretations and from then on the ideas fractaled and varied from person to person and region to region. One has to study several schools and texts of Buddhism to grasp what the central ideas are and that they have possibly evolved quite a lot since Siddartha existed.

To understand this central core of Buddhism, we should certainly branch our way into the other beliefs at the time to help us grasp what is useful and what is not. History should help us out in this case. Scholars refer to the time of both Buddhism and Taoism as the Axial age, around 500 BCE to 0 BCE, the point in society where some shifted from nomadic peoples and farmers to live in cities, and new ideas were discussed and kicked around from people all over the world. This was the time that the Greeks began their philosophy, studies of the stars were in full swing and China and India both had their share of philosophers. As a philosopher in India or Greece you would often travel around and debate other philosophers and gain prestige for beating each other in debates.

Each area had a different way of going about philosophy. Aristotle had asked Alexander the Great to bring back 100 Gurus from India to understand their philosophy, but Alexander died before being able to do so, and that event failed. Kublai Khan sent a letter with Marco Polo to the pope to send 100 learned men of the cloth to China, but the Pope died and the letter never was delivered. Imagine how much different the world would have been had these fields of philosophy merged, the way that Greek and Indian mathematics merged in the library of Baghdad to give us Al-gebra and other synchronized ideas.

Part 1: The Evolution of Buddhism

Buddhism is a child of Hinduism with influences from other Indian religions attempting to escape the reincarnation cycle. Without understanding these other religious concepts that Buddhism was birthed in, the philosophy will not make as much sense and it will not be as easy to separate the religion it was swimming in from the philosophy.

"It is good to tame the mind, which is difficult to hold in and flighty, rushing wherever it listeth; a tamed mind brings happiness." - Buddha (Dhammapada Verse 35)

Hinduism

Hinduism, just like everything in the old sanskrit language, has a lot of nuanced meanings. It refers to a national religion, ethnic traditions, a secular collection of polytheistic faiths, many schools of philosophy, and a slowly declining caste system. Hinduism is full of contradictions and paradoxes and if one were to try to point it out to a Hindu, they will agree with you as if it is obvious, but then be confused as to why that matters.

Hinduism is possibly the second oldest continuously practiced religion in the world, with the first being a 70,000 year-old Botswana folk religion involving the worship of a stone serpent (Minkel, 2006). Hinduism's longevity is in part thanks to the flexibility of its practice, and how it spreads and evolves in different regions. There are some regions that have rituals and songs that are so old, linguists could not figure out what the songs meant for their rituals, but biologists were able to discover that the songs mimicked animal sounds that must have been heard in very ancient times(Staal, 1985).

Hinduism is treated with varying degrees of passion and importance in India, some viewing it as a cultural set of enjoyable holidays, and some taking it very seriously, sometimes by swimming in the extremely polluted Ganges river. Quite often they will build gorgeous elaborate Idols that the avatar

god will come and inhabit and live with them for a few days, which they treat with reverence and honor and then at the end of the holiday they burn the idol to release the deity to go do things out in the world.

Hindus believe that the world and humans in general are eternal by nature. The world goes through cycles of birth, growth,

if you were evil you are born into a lower caste or as an animal. The caste system is a somewhat later addition to Hinduism, which fits some bills of division of labor and rationalizing why the rich are rich and therefore better, and the poor are poor because in their past life they were horrible people and deserve it. The caste system laws are slowly changing and people of low castes are slowly working their way up to equality in the nation, but with much of the same civil rights problems as in the US.

There are many schools of thought in Hinduism, including an atheistic one, however one of the more modern, prominent and binding philosophies put forth by the Bhagavad Gita and later Madame Blavatsky, the mother or the occult and influencer of Gandhi, is that Brahma is one deity, but there is no way for the human mind to grasp the greatness and wonder and complicated mind of Brahma, so there are 33 million avatars, each with their own personality that are just fragments of Brahma. Some are vengeful or angry, some are kind and loving, some heap prosperity, and some bring famine.

The idea of the Brahma, broken up into individual avatars, can also be supported by neurology. A psychological study had people in an MRI(magnetic resonance imager) think of certain individuals. The idea was to focus on specific, separate individuals. When people were asked to think about God, the same areas lit up. What is also

and destruction. We are currently in the age right before the age of destruction. Everything that happens may suck now but we will travel through an age in another life when things are better. Thanks to Golden Age Syndrome where the brain remembers bad things happening currently and easily forgets a large number of bad memories in the past to help you avoid depression and suicide, it's very easy to think we are always near the end times and most cultures believed we were in some form of end time.

Reincarnation, also called Samsara, is a personal cycle. If you are a good person in your life you are reborn as a higher caste, interesting is when people are asked what god thinks, the MRI scans match up exactly to the areas of the brain that lit up when they were asked what they think(Kapogiannis, 2009). An added side note, when people are asked what god thinks, it matches exactly the area of the brain when asked what they think(Epley, 2009).

Understanding some of the basics of Hinduism is required to put the religion of Buddhism into perspective. Parts of Hinduism such as Samsara were initially essential ideas of Buddhism but depending on the region and local religion that adopted it, Samsara has either been incorporated or dropped entirely in place of local ancestor worship or spirits moving on into the afterlife. It is why analyzing the core of Buddhism as a philosophy is essential, as there are so many religious denominations of Buddhism that it rivals Christianity and Islam by the same percentage of its believers.

Jainism and Asceticism

Jainism is a religion rivaling Buddhism in antiquity. The Buddha was just one of many wise men seeking and claiming enlightenment. Like Buddhism, which believes that there were many Buddhas who have discovered enlightenment but then the secrets were forgotten and a new Buddha came along and rediscovered it, Jains have the Tirthankaras or Enlightened figures of which their latest one is the 24th in the cycle

named Mahavira, and they will reach enlightenment and end the cycle of samsara. Jain monastics, renunciants, and devout householders take five main vows known as vratas, outlined in their oldest surviving text, the Acaranga Sūtra: ahimsā ("non-violence"), satya ("truth"), asteya ("not stealing"), brahmacharya ("celibacy or chastity"), and aparigraha ("non-attachment"). If this sounds familiar to anyone who has studied Buddhism before, it is because Buddhists also follow some of these but with a bit more nuance. Jains take this to an extreme of a vegetarian or even vegan lifestyle and will

go out of their way to not even step on bugs or harm some plants to get their food if that plant will die from harvesting. If a plant drops a food however, that is a gift, not a theft.

Violence is never permissible no matter the reason. You will lose spiritual merit setting you back dramatically from reaching your goal of enlightenment. No other religion has taken non-violence to the extreme that Jainism has. Though throughout history when faced with threat they have justified some cases such as monks protecting nuns using violence.

The many-sided reality is another Jain idea, using the Taoist idea that language was a flawed way to attempt to describe reality or the Tao. Jains taught that all statements are true and valid. While Buddha taught to never speak in certainty, Mahavira taught his followers to accept that a statement both is and is not true with a qualified "perhaps."

"Non-attachment" is another idea that Jains hold strongly. Lay Jains should own as little as possible and only what they earned in an honest way. In addition, Jain texts mention that "attachment to possessions" (parigraha) is of two kinds: attachment to internal possessions (ābhyantara parigraha), and attachment to external possessions (bāhya parigraha). For internal possessions, Jainism identifies four key passions of the mind (kashaya): anger, pride (ego), deceitfulness, and greed. In addition to the four passions of the mind, the remaining ten internal passions are: wrong belief, the three sex-passions (male sex-passion, female sex-passion, neuter sex-passion), and the six defects (laughter, like, dislike, sorrow, fear, disgust).

Ascetics monks and nuns own no possessions and are homeless and without family. These are people who believe they could gain knowledge and enlightenment by subjecting their bodies to the most extremes of abuse. Self- harm, whipping, starvation, uncomfortable yoga poses held for hours or days, extreme heat, cold, nakedness, insect bites you name it. However, Jains were not the only ascetics of the time. Many other branches existed, each trying to discover enlightenment and escape samsara. Some would hold themselves in very hard to achieve yoga poses for hours or days on end in hopes of clearing and purifying their minds. Some would whip themselves, and physically harm themselves. Gautama Siddhartha studied under many such ascetics

and ended up almost drowning because he nearly starved himself to death. Asceticism played a huge part in Buddhistic thinking and its ultimate metamorphosis.

The Life of the Buddha

Gautama Siddhartha, according to Indian Buddhist lore, was the most recent Buddha. There have been many Buddhas, each one through the ages. When people forget the last one's teachings, a new one rises.

Gautama Siddartha, as much as we can tell, probably existed, sometime between the 6th and 4th century BCE, and taught Buddhism. How much of what his initial philosophy matches with the current philosophy or how much of his story is fact is impossible to know. He wrote nothing down and allegedly had 32 disciples that each opened their own schools of thought after his death, each with slightly competing interpretations of their master's teachings. This does not make the current philosophy any less valid, however it may have not been the philosophy of the original Buddha with the centuries of evolution.

The universal mythos of the Buddha is that he was born Gautama Siddhartha, the prince of a great king in modern day north-east India. The king asked the soothsayers what kind of child his son would be. All but one said he would be either one of two things, a great conquering king, or the greatest and wisest ascetic to ever live. One

dismissed the dual claim and just said bluntly that the child would be an ascetic and was punished politically for it, pointing out the reality that telling the truth to powerful people is politically dangerous and will rarely be rewarded.

The king of course wanted his son to be a great king, not some shabby suffering ascetic, no matter how wise. The soothsayers told the king that the best way to ensure that would happen was to make sure his son never knew about sickness, age, death and asceticism. The king made him 3 great pleasure palaces, and ensured his son was only surrounded by young healthy people. All sick people were removed from his sight. How exactly the king planned his son to be a great ruler without understanding these major important factors of humanity is confusing, but it made sense at the time for this mythos.

Gautama had a great time growing up, thinking the world was amazing, the fat buddha people think of most often is sometimes considered the pre-enlightenment, naïve, happy Gautama of this time. Other people claim it was a generic representation of a happy buddha or another specific

Buddha made happy by his unconditional love or balance of thoughts and tranquility. However, he desired his freedom and hated being locked away like any young person and managed to escape the palace. There, for the first time, he encountered a sick person, an old person, and a dead person. He required people to explain it to him. Some claim it was a person who knew who he was, and the gods forced him to tell the truth, some didn't, some say the entire presentation was just the gods themselves in disguise. The shock of these truths that we all would be sick, old and die was profound to the young man.

Lastly, he saw an ascetic with his begging bowl and asked what the man was doing. He was told that this man had given up everything to learn the secrets of life and the afterlife. The prince returned to the palace and with much thought about the paradigm shift in his reality. He decided to leave the palace and become an ascetic. He could no longer live in this illusion of perfection and eternal youth. He had a wife and newborn son but saw neither prior to leaving in fear that seeing them would break his resolve to leave. He left the palace, his wife and his newborn child for good, ready to find the meaning of life.

Gautama begins his training

Gautama sought out ascetics. Pleasure didn't seem to bring enlightenment so extreme denial of pleasure might. Gautama studied under them and over time he had disciples of his own, teaching the art of asceticism, however he never felt like he was getting anywhere. He never felt like he had figured out how to escape death, reality, samsara or even figure out what was the point to life and existence.

During his high pain or discomfort sessions he would lose all focus on reality, either from an endorphin rush or the intense focus on the pain, but once it was over, he came back to reality and was still living in this miserable world. His once well-

© Anson Chappell

manicured and well-fed body looked like a boney dried up husk of a being. And he was still neither happy nor content with life, just as he had not been in the palace surrounded by servants and pleasures. He was always trying to attain enlightenment and felt like it was always just outside his grasp.

Any time he did something to sustain himself, a simple pleasure such as eating a grain of rice to ensure he could keep himself alive, he discovered that it came with the price of intense guilt; something we see even now with many people suffering from eating disorders like anorexia and bulimia.. If he did not meditate enough or he felt physically "good," it brought him guilt. At one point he had himself so starved and weakened that he fell into a river and almost drowned.

This was the turning point that changed his approach. How could he ever attain enlightenment if he couldn't even stay alive? Gautama had to do a full reboot on how he approached the subject. A local woman brought him food, something that was very common in hopes of increasing their karma. Normally he would have eaten from the offering over a very long time, and it would have spoiled. Instead he ate the whole meal without guilt.

Mother Teresa had a similar story when she first came to India. Nuns have very simple meal rations they live off of. She saw many people in poverty and gave away her lunch. Later in the day she nearly passed out from lack of food from their rigorous work. From that day on she learned the lesson that you must first care for yourself before you can care for others. Sadly like The Guru, she was also something of a scam artist but even worse as she perpetuated suffering where it shouldn't have been.

From this point on Gautama decided to try a completely different method. He sat under a Bodhi tree and decided to meditate until he gained enlightenment. In fact, the term Bodhi means "enlightenment" or "awakening." No pain, no self-denial. Instead he used a simple breathing technique he had noticed as a child, focusing on the inflow of air into his abdomen and the release of air. This distracted one from other thoughts of the past or future or other concepts and allowed a complete focus on just the moment, just the here and now. It is worth mentioning that according to some legends he invented this breathing technique at the age of 7.

Which comes back to how we have evolved our understanding of the use of meditation with modern psychology. One of the best ways to figure out a problem is to let your mind rest. Being overly focused on one thing can lock in the neural networks so you are too focused on one way of thinking. This prevents you from finding new avenues to solve the problem. By focusing on just breathing and being in the moment the mind can do a relaxed reset allowing

for fresh ideas. It is why many will claim that praying allowed them to find a missing item. Praying, like meditation, relaxes the mind. Quite often the act of praying lets the mind relax enough to think about the problem in a different context and tackle the problem from a different angle.

As for Gautama, after 49 days of meditating he was said to have hit upon what he called the 4 truths of reality and what is referred to as the 8 fold path.

What is Enlightenment?

Throughout the book so far we have referred to the concept of enlightenment. While it was and is still a term used to discuss a method of breaking the cycle of Samsara or rebirth, it's a lot more complex. Bodhi or Enlightenment is a state of awareness. Bodhi is an abstract word meaning knowledge, wisdom or awakened intellect.

Most of the Pali texts were translated to English during the Victorian Era and there were a few translational issues that create a lot of misconceptions on Bodhi to this day in the common understanding. Bodhi refers to an awakening to reality, a state of cultivated mindfulness, and the ability to purge unhelpful and harmful desires from your mind. Eliminate all attachments, freeing you from the prison of these harmful or useless desires.

Unfortunately thanks to a mix of confused translation, black and white ideals of salvation from evil that bled over from Christianity, and pop culture understanding of Eastern mysticism, the idea of "enlightenment" translated over to mean: A state where all desire is eliminated, one who has complete control of all their desires and their mind. One who can see all the world with clarity and has unlimited wisdom as humanity naturally has wisdom, they just have to drop their desires. They are essentially superhuman at this point and will automatically break Samsara and can never fall from this state once they have entered.

This superhuman reverence and misunderstanding has been taken advantage of by many "Buddhist Masters," especially in the West, where their students will blindly let their "masters" abuse and manipulate them, thinking they are obviously wise and enlightened so there must be an enlightened reason for treating them in such a way that their unenlightened minds couldn't possibly imagine. The abuse is obviously for their own good so they accept it with gratitude believing they are being done a great service by this god-like being by passing on this wisdom and accept their abuses with gratitude. (Horgan, 2011)

It's for this reason that "Enlightenment" is a loaded word and many buddhists prefer to use the word "awakened", or just "bodhi" to eliminate the god-like feel to it. One who is awakened also has not eliminated all of their desires, just the ones that are harmful or no longer helpful, like eliminating clutter so they have more mental energy to focus on more important things. They believe they have eliminated all of their attachments, so they don't double the level of suffering reality naturally causes by allowing their unchecked desire to make the problem even worse.

The Teachings of the Buddha

It was in the Deer Park that the freshly enlightened Buddha now presented his new ideas to his fellow ascetics. It changed the entire direction of history and ways of thinking for millennia to come. His ideas about the existence of reality and life was quite a dramatic shift from ideas at the time.

The 4 noble truths consisted of the following:

1. Reality is suffering.

There is actually a more nuanced Sanskrit word Dakha, which includes "disappointment." An example of this Truth might be when you wake up in the morning and realize you don't have more time to sleep, you are disappointed. Life will often disappoint you. Life is also suffering. Perhaps there are physical or mental pains that make you suffer. They won't cease. And the truth is that this is just a part of life. All sentient beings have stress, because of our necessary drive toward pleasure and avoidance of pain.

2. Suffering is caused by attachment.

When you expect something good to happen and it doesn't, you are disappointed. When you crave something you can't

have, you suffer, even if it is just the tiniest bit. Your brain's reward pathway runs on dopamine. If you have a high threshold of expectation, your brain prepares itself for the stimulus to provide the dopamine, just as smelling food prepares your mind and salivary glands to eat the food. However, if you find out you don't get to have that stimulus, the mind has lowered its dopamine output, which can reduce happiness to much lower levels than if you were never expecting the stimulus in the first place.

It is why when trying to clean up your diet from sugars and white carbs, one has to go for about a month without them to reboot the dopamine rewards one gets from junk food. After going without, sugary items that used to be normal for you will taste way too sweet and you will need way less of it to get the same dopamine response.

Just like with suffering, desire, attachment or Tanhā in Pali, it is more nuanced and not a perfect translation either. It can mean thirst, desire, greed or longing. This desire is caused by defilements or the three poisons, Kleshas, or negative states of mind that cloud our thinking that we will discuss later.

There are 3 kinds of Tanhā:

Kāma-tanhā (sensual pleasures craving): This involves craving sense objects or sensory pleasures. These are also emotional pleasures like the feeling of power and wealth as well as attachment to ideas or ideals, views, opinions or beliefs.

Bhava-tanhā (craving for being): This is not only a craving for life and perhaps immortality, but a craving for an attachment to identity or belonging.

Vibhava-tanhā (craving for

non-existence):This idea is the craving to not experience unpleasant things in your life both this and the next life. This can lead to not only suicides but risk aversion preventing change from happening that could be positive. I feel like this form of Tanhā is often overlooked by Westernized versions of Buddhist teaching, especially ones watered down to sell to the middle class.

Desire is a prime motivator in humans, and is required to do anything in life. Attachment on the other hand is when you are so tied to your desire that you can never have peace at all. However thanks to the Western concepts of good and evil that many Eastern philosophies lack, the idea of desire is often displayed as always bad or evil and something to avoid and eliminate at all costs.

This attachment to eliminate all desire can create unrealistic expectations, creating its own set of Tanhā that it was meant to eliminate.

3. Eliminating desire eliminates suffering.

If you don't expect or desire anything, you will not suffer. This sounds a bit strange but if you had no desires for things getting better, you would never be disappointed. We can look back on the example above: eliminating the desire for sugar eliminates the suffering. After going without, sugary items that used to be normal for you will taste way too sweet and you will need way less of it to get the same dopamine response. Like with cocaine, your brain always needs more sugar and carbs over time to get the same dopamine hit to the point that some become food addicts, causing massive weight gain. By going through a period of cycles of self-denial can you reset your brain to get a lot of dopamine out of a little bit of sweet or white carbs.

If you accept death and pain, it will hurt you less. Fear of death is much worse than actual death and if you are mentally fighting pain and not accepting it, your mind has even more strain on it than it would normally have, causing more suffering.

Remember that suffering of Dakha is not unpleasantness from an external source but all from an internal source. Even so, suffering from desire, if it drives motivation in ways that are good, can be worth it, just as suffering from a painful surgery can be worthwhile in the long term. The goal is to eliminate the worthless or even toxic desires, just like with clutter. Having too much takes more time and work and takes away from your well being instead of enriching it.

4. Following the Eight-Fold Path

Psychologists have found in studies that the happiest people have lower expectations. These are not cynical people; they just don't expect very much and enjoy things that do go right (Schultz, 2014). Upon release from desire, suffering will go away, as will reality. To some in Buddhism this is a release from Samsara or reincarnation called Nirvana. To some it is just a state of liberation from pointless suffering.

Buddha prescribed the 8-fold path to accomplish reaching this state.

they are organized are different depending on which source you get it from. Here they are divided by type.

-Moral Virtue

Right action divides in meaning depending on the Buddhist branch that were pro-sex or anti-sex, or pro-alcohol or perhaps even staunchly vegan. What decides the "right" action ultimately is decided by you.

Right speech involves avoiding lying, rudeness and gossiping

Right livelihood involves not engaging in trades that sell poison, weapons, slaves, meat and liquor.

-Meditation

Right effort involves remaining guarded and on watch so that your mind does not reach an unwholesome state. It includes being aware of your senses and how you might react in a state where you no longer have control of your desires.

Right mindfulness involves being ever aware and ever mindful of the teachings and elements of the Buddha.

Right concentration will lead to a form of tranquility or pleasure from finding the truth and meditation that in turn will lead to a stage of neither pleasure nor pain.

The 8-fold path

Right action

Right speech

Right livelihood

Right effort

Right mindfulness

Right concentration

Right intention

Right view

Let's break these down a little here. The way

-Wisdom and insight

The right view is a complex discussion that is rooted deeply in skepticism. There's no room for delusions, only truth for the sake of truth, no matter the pain it would cause to a person with desire.

The right intention tries to ensure that you are doing good deliberately for the sake of the good. Often people will do good for the feeling it gives them, or even the praise the action may cause. That feeling is an after effect that will happen regardless. Craving that feeling can often lead to doing something you think is good but could end up harmful or even a waste of action. It must be with the right intention.

Understanding these allows you to understand what is referred to as the "3 Marks of Existence."

1. Impermanence:

The only constant is change. Every time you feel you have a handle on reality, it will throw you something new whether you chose it or not. It requires one to be content with change and to expect adversity and prepare as best as one can without worrying about it.

Much like the weather, change is most certainly going to happen so you might as well accept it and deal with it. Worrying about it makes the pain of change even worse. Change can also occur in very small ways to the point that you do not notice it unless you are very conscious and self-aware. Go with the flow of reality; trying to resist will cause wasted energy, although if you are aware enough, you can direct the flow to your benefit.

"Life is what happens when you are busy making other plans." - Cartoonist Allen Saunders

2. Not-self

This is a concept that involves giving up our perceived Identity. While growing up in rural Indiana, changing one's self was viewed as not being "true to yourself." There was a sense of selling out and dishonesty. Of course, the real self and ideal self are two completely different creatures, and when they come together in the sharp focus of perception it creates cognitive dissonance. Your brain will do anything to rationalize any disparity between the two, so you won't have to have the pain self-awareness brings.

Letting go of your perception of self is essentially acknowledging your real self, and seeing yourself for all the flaws you have that you hide from yourself. Only when you can see the real you can you see all the flaws you kept hidden from yourself and then you can begin to fix and change your true self toward your ideal self. Achieving Not-Self requires resisting desire to be the ideal self. One must look at all their flaws and accept them for what they are and realize that these flaws are all part of being human. However, with this non-judgmental assessment you've made, you have the power to change your real self and mold it into something closer to your ideal self.

3. Suffering

Suffering or disappointment is a natural part of reality. It will always be with you. Anticipation readies the brain for sensation, lack of that sensation causes more pain than had the anticipation never occurred. Anticipation of desire is a way out of suffering and disappointment, which requires training to drop one's ego and their idea of self. But remember that the power is always in you. It requires eliminating mental clutter and baggage that is holding you back.

Are you tired of math yet? Because with the 4 Noble Truths, the 8-Fold Path and the 3 Marks of Existence, there are also 5 Trainings that Buddhists must undergo to reach enlightenment.

The 5 Trainings to Attain Enlightenment:
1. Realization that suffering is caused by doing harm, so harm no living thing
2. Realizing that suffering comes from taking what is not freely given
3. Do not engage in sexual relationships that cause harm to self or others
4. Recognize that unmindful speech causes harm to others. Truthfulness can cause harm as well
5. Recognize that suffering comes from greedy consumption

Next are the 3 Poisons, which are the 3 causes of all that we in the West call "sin."

You might say these are the sources of all human evil, when you think about it.

The 3 Poisons

1. Moha. Illusion, delusion or ignorance.

Socrates believed people were evil because they just didn't understand things. If a person knew drinking alcohol was bad for them, and really understood, they would stop. That sadly is not enough. If knowledge was available to all, we may be able to eliminate a third of the evil in the world. However, knowledge requires a lot of work, not only to push the brain through boredom, which is essentially the muscle pain from working out your brain which allows it to grow, but also dealing with the rough paradigm shifts in perspective that learning brings. This requires a lot of effort. This is why humanity won't ever fully have the knowledge, which ties well into:

2. Dvesha. Aversion or laziness.

Confuscious thought that man would be good if they just stopped being lazy and worked hard at everything, both learning and doing. However, laziness is hardwired into us for energy conservation and what one may call laziness, another may call self-care or even mental health issues. The act of overcoming legitimate laziness could possibly eliminate two-thirds of all evil in the world, which hopefully would help eliminate:

3. Raga. Greed, attachment or addiction.

Buddha realized that attachment was a form of addiction. We love dopamine rushes, but it causes emotional pain and suffering when we expect a dopamine rush and it doesn't come, as explained earlier. Because of this we have addictions to food, drugs, tobacco, alcohol and unsafe sex, to name a few. We even have an addiction to the other two poisons or the extreme opposite of the other two poisons. We can be addicted to our delusions and learning they are false hurts, so instead of pushing through

39

the pain and accepting it, we dig ourselves deeper into our own ignorance and delusion. We do everything we can to hide ourselves from the truth.

We can also go the opposite way and break delusions too soon, causing us to be unable to cope with reality. Growing up I was addicted to learning every terrible thing I could about reality, thinking it made me more empathic, but what it instead did was make my depression much worse, crippling me from doing anything. This ensured that instead of doing a little to help ease the suffering of others I instead had no energy to help anyone and just hurt myself.

It's a journey, not a destination. You will never be done. One must always be working on fixing one's delusions and ignorance but at a pace that is healthy to one's mental health. Mostly because emotions aren't rational and breaking some of your prior beliefs require a mourning process to fully let go of the bad idea, especially if we feel it is a core of our identity.

We are also addicted to laziness. Some of this is due to evolution. In nature, energy consumption is a numbers game. You must take in at least as much as you put out. To acquire more energy and successfully reproduce, we must put out more energy so it's a constant tradeoff game. To successfully pass on your genes, you must take shortcuts, and the mind has to do its best to create incentives to conserve energy. Doing as little as possible is the default state of the brain unless given a good enough motivation.

We can also be addicted to the opposite of laziness, often called being a "workaholic." For many, getting into the swing of being productive is hard so putting the brakes on work after finally getting to that point and resting is too much of an effort. However, our work suffers as often do our relationships if we don't take time to rest, and it requires letting go and slowing down to gain new perspectives.

An addiction to emotions is one of the most difficult to overcome. Emotions tint your perception of the world and your perception may not be accurate or it may be overgeneralized. It's like being addicted to a drug but you are being dosed constantly without your consent. One can get addicted to every emotion, even unpleasant ones like sadness or self-loathing.

So the theory stands that without the 3 Poisons, there would be no evil. But because each causes the other, there will always be some degree of evil in the world. The point is to slowly, ever so slightly, make the world have less evil in it. Zeno's paradox, but always taking a half-step forward.

There are 7 factors to awakening

1. Mindfulness
2. Investigation or curiosity about reality
3. Energy or determination and effort
4. Joy or rapture which includes emotional states such as getting goosebumps, short period of joyful emotion, intense joyful emotions, emotions that make you feel light and emotions or joy that is also overwhelming
5. Relaxation and tranquility of body and mind
6. Concentration
7. Equanimity or to accept reality as it is, not craving it to be different or aversion to thinking about its negatives.

There are 4 stages awakening:

1. One is secluded from sensuality and other unwholesome mental factors, and along with rapture, right effort and discursive thought,

one can move to the next stage
2. This is a state of rapture, and non-sensual pleasure from concentration. Unification of awareness and time without discursive thought. Inner tranquility
3. This is a stage of equanimity and disconnection from useless and negative attachments. Being mindful and alert, and sensing pleasure with the body.
4. When one reaches pure equanimity and mindfulness. One is experiencing neither pleasure nor pain.

Bodhisattva

The word Bodhisattva refers to a sentient beings or sattva that has developed bodhi or enlightenment — and therefore possess the bodhisattva's psyche; one who works to develop and exemplify the loving-kindness (metta), compassion (karuna), empathetic joy (mudita) and equanimity (upekkha). These four virtues are the four divine abodes, called Brahmavihara (illimitables). This is akin to the Christian saint of someone who has been born again and is living their life through Jesus Christ and doing everything to emulate him.

Part 2: The Buddha and Bias

One day a man came to the Buddha and asked, "Is there a God?" The Buddha looked at him for a minute and then said "Yes." The man left, looking frustrated.

Later that day, another man came and asked the same question. "Is there a God?" The Buddha looked at him for a minute and then said "No." The man left, very disappointed.

Lastly at the end of the day, a man came and said,

"Say something about God." The Buddha looked at him for a minute then, smiling, began to meditate. They meditated together for half an hour. The man was very touched, thanked him, and left with wide eyes.

Later that night, his close disciple and older cousin Ananda could not contain his confusion on the subject any longer. He knew his master didn't believe in God. What was happening?

"First off, those questions were not your questions and so those answers were also not for you or anyone else. Thinking in absolutes is very dangerous and is one of your big hindrances. Life is relative."

"The first man was an absolutely certain atheist. I could tell that he wanted me to confirm his belief he held onto very strongly with emotion so that nothing would change his mind. So, I told him, 'yes.' In some unexplored area we do not see or do not know there could be a god. You can say with absolute certainty that there is no God when you have explored all of reality, but until then, you can never say anything with complete certainty. I had to shatter that ego and certainty and put some doubt into his thinking. That is why that answer was for him."

"The second man was just as stupid and stubborn as the first man, except the polar opposite. He was certain there was a

God and wanted my support to confirm it. It does not matter what belief you have that is idiotic, it only matters what the truth is. So, I told him 'no' for the same reason as I told the other man 'yes.'

"The third man came to me with no belief, no certainty and an open mind. He was not here for support or to find something to believe in, nor was he prejudiced in any way. His curiosity was about what my personal experiences were. Unlike the other two, he was a sane, intelligent man. With this

kind of innocence and openness, words are meaningless. I cannot say 'yes,' I cannot say 'no,' so silence is the only answer. So, I closed my eyes and remained silent. I was correct about him and when I closed my eyes, so did he, taking my meaning to be 'be silent, go in'. He remained with me for a half hour in silence and received the answer that God is not a theory or a belief you have to be for or against. That is why he thanked me for the answer. He received the answer that silence is divine, and to be silent is to be godly, and there is no other God but silence. He found that answer. I did not give it to him. I just lead by example."

One of the greatest teachings of the Buddha involved questioning your own prejudices and looking and embracing the uncomfortable truths of life and learning to be content with it. The Buddha stumbled on some very important ideas that only came into common practice and understanding in the sciences in the last 60 years.

Cognitive biases

Cognitive biases are the unintentional favoring of personally believed or favored information and outcomes. Biases are something we all have and suffer from. They are unintentional, and most of us are entirely unaware that we have them. The brain is hardwired to make natural shortcuts, which works for the most part in keeping us alive but doesn't function well at ascertaining the truth. Cognitive Biases are not intentional; one can believe they are 100% honest about a study being done, but when an outside observer with no emotional ties or benefits to them analyzes the information, they may find very critical flaws in the argument or idea.

Bias works the same way magic tricks work. Your brain is having flaws exploited, and when it's pointed out to you as to how it works, your brain is still limited so the trick will continue to appear to be magic. Just like how a TV screen appears to be moving pictures as opposed to rapidly changing still images.

Your brain convinces you that something is true even when it is completely false. Every single one of us has biases that we are trapped by. It causes us to give inaccurate assumptions about reality. If we are not raised with the understanding of bias, many of us have the emotional feeling of "knowing," which feels almost spiritual. The sense of knowing and understanding, seeing patterns and connections that aren't really there, can create a euphoric experience.

Just how strongly this feeling of knowing can affect someone can be shown in a psychological disease that is called Cotard's syndrome, which is a rare neurophysiological condition where a patient is convinced that they are dead and a walking corpse. Any attempt to try and convince the person using logic and evidence will be

flipped back around, dismissed, or rationalized. If you tell the victim that they have a pulse, instead of saying, "Oh, I must be alive then," they will instead take the opposite approach and say, "Oh, that's evidence that dead people have pulses."

There was a 69 year old Japanese man who had a brain infarction which caused him to acquire this syndrome. When he recovered, even when he understood and admitted that it was because of the disease that he believed he was dead, the train of thought and world view his brain was in and that comfortable certainty of knowing had him continue to believe, rationalize, and profess that he had been dead but now wasn't. As a side note He also was convinced that Kim Jong-Il was a patient at the hospital. Once a brain is convinced of something it is very hard for someone to reverse their logic(Nishio 2012).

The biases are often categorized into 3 groups.

-The first is called the Belief, decision-making and behavioral biases.

The **Dunning-Kruger effect** is an

example of this concept. The Dunning Krueger effect is the concept that people who are experts are less likely to think they know as much as they do, while the people who know very little about the subject tend to assume they know a lot more about it than they do. As stated in the Abstract of the original study "Across 4 studies, the authors found that participants scoring in the bottom quartile on tests of humor, grammar, and logic grossly overestimated their test performance and ability. Although their test scores put them in the 12th percentile, they estimated themselves to be in the 62nd." It was only once they increased their own knowledge that they were able to know just how much they didn't know. (Kruger, 1999).

-The second group is called Social Biases.

Paul Piff ran an experiment where he gave one person a bunch of extra money at the beginning of a game of a monopoly and another person the same amount. As they began to play, the person who fully knew they had been given an advantage began boasting and truly believing that it was their superior skill and actions that actually made them win so well, and could have done just as well without the advantages (Solman, 2013). This is an extreme example of the **Self-serving bias,** where one claims more responsibility for successes than failures.

The final group is called Memory Biases.

Another example of cognitive bias is **Misinformation bias** where you lose details over time because of interference from post event information. This is exemplified by the Challenger study. It was a typical memory study that had people write down things around the time that the Challenger exploded. Things like where they were, what they were feeling, and so on. Years later they wrote down their memories and recalled that day, then they could compare their answers with their original one. Memory is not a snapshot; it is constantly changing and being rewritten as new memories come along. The very odd thing about this experiment was that when their new memories didn't match their original memories, they just couldn't believe it. They would rationalize it and in some cases even go as far as to convince themselves that their past self must have been lying (Neisser & Harsch, 1992).

Brain power and accuracy are things people take very seriously and are very important to people. If your memory doesn't match someone else's, and you go looking for evidence and show them they remembered something wrong, it causes a surge of irrational emotions. Losing that feeling of knowing is very painful and adds a sense of helplessness. It's like an attack on their identity of having a good memory. People also take it as a personal insult when you point out that their memory was faulty because

they feel it indicates that they are stupid, or not as intelligent as they believed themselves to be. The reality is that we all have fluid memories, and it requires meticulous techniques that many would consider almost obsessive to continually rewrite your memories with a low error rate.

The Biases Expanded

A cognitive bias is an unconscious phenomenon that we all struggle with; the majority of humanity are completely unaware of. It persists because there is no evolutionary pressure to fix this problem. We can still reproduce with these biases, even when we are completely ignorant of actual reality. These biases can be evolutionarily advantageous if your sense of knowing gives you confidence even if in reality you have no real reason to be confident about your feeling of knowing. As the feeling of knowing is so overwhelming, euphoric and spiritual, we can actually repeat this emotional stimulation in a lab with drugs and other altered states.

If you are raised in a religion and are taught the language of the religion, and you have a feeling of knowing, the only language you have to describe this feeling is in religious language. Your brain reverses the order of memory, so it feels like you knew before you were taught.

Scientists learn to ignore their feelings of correctness more often than the lay person until the evidence is backed up by science, to avoid confirmation bias. This idea and attempt to practice delaying "knowing" is a major part of Buddhism. Your beliefs about reality are part of your identity and your own ego. When you learn something new that goes counter to what you hold dear, that causes suffering. So, many will do whatever it takes to prevent having to believe new facts. Biases provide everything you need to reject new ideas and to hold onto your initial beliefs that soothe your ego.

This of course doesn't mean anyone is completely free of biases, but scientists are much more likely to have less of them in their field. Ignoring that feeling of knowing is hard and painful because certainty feels so good. The neural networks in the brain become more complex as time goes on, making it a lot harder to drop a belief the longer the belief is held. If you have only been in a religion for 2 years, it's much easier to leave it than someone who has been involved in a religious practice for 40 years.

Belief, decision-making and behavioral biases.

Status quo bias is when the brain makes one believe that the new change needed to accept a new idea is not for the better. It prevents the brain from changing because of the work, sacrifices and stresses needed to change their mind on a topic. Going back to the discussion on laziness, the brain is evolved to conserve energy and if the brain can convince itself that effort should not be put into something, it won't.

There was a man who came to our local Center For Inquiry, a national free-thinking organization, who was a theist in the loosest sense of the word. He was not a biblical literalist, and he didn't believe in the majority of the bible or the theology and saw most of it as metaphor. However, he had two things that he claimed that if he could be convinced that these two things weren't true, he would have to become an atheist.

The first was his belief that some biblical prophecies had shown themselves to be fulfilled. The other was his beliefs that there were conclusive studies that intercessory prayer worked when praying to the Christian god. The great thing about the Center is that we had a lot of educated people in many different fields. People with expertise in history, archeology, statistics and other backgrounds who genuinely wanted to find out his evidence, but when he presented some it was so easy to destroy without even trying. We exhausted ourselves trying to do unbiased research to try and explain to him why his arguments and evidence were flawed. And the funny thing is, he agreed with everything we said, every piece of evidence we threw at him he agreed with, but when you saw him the next day, he still repeated the same arguments.

He never really got around to saying anything of substance either. He continued in logical and rhetorical loops, saying that his studies and research were double-blind, skeptical and scientific but wouldn't actually get to the meat of the evidence so it was hard to pin him down and argue against his position. He seemed to just want to convince us and himself that he was a skeptic by saying phrases that skeptics use without actually applying it to his own beliefs. We eventually gave up. His brain wanted to believe what it wanted to believe, and it was doing everything including insulting us for not being skeptical, and taking a condescending and patronizing tone in an attempt to feel

superior for his beliefs.

We later discovered that this man apparently had a disease that was potentially fatal, and through his use of prayer, he convinced himself he had avoided and/or survived a brush with death.. Death is the one time when the rules of logic and reality no longer apply, and the origin of the belief might have very well occurred, like the man with Cotard's syndrome. Now that the potential cause of his beliefs had passed, his brain still did not want to put in the effort to change its train of thought.

Religion seems to almost be written with natural biases in mind, as they use the phrase "evidence only comes to believers." If you don't believe, then God is not going to bother to show you the evidence. This is very backward thinking, but it makes complete sense in their minds.

Of course, if you believe something unquestioningly, your bias will select only evidence you agree with. That is the very nature of belief.

There is no reason to feel judged or stupid for holding a bias, though after the fact you probably will, as these biases are naturally evolved into us. All the greatest and smartest people hold biases, some biases even shown to be pretty dumb, but they are blinded by their own neurology to them. We all have delusions. But being aware of the biases that you are programmed for can allow you to get practice in building mental constructs to combat these biases and get much closer to reality and empirical truth. Things like maintaining a sliver of doubt for any idea that one may hold helps a lot.

Many Atheists I know are very proud of themselves because they were able to overcome their religious biases. They see themselves as superior to people who haven't, while many remain completely oblivious that they still are slaves to their own biases. Becoming an Atheist is just one of many possible first steps to becoming anti-biased. Anti-bias or the more often abused label, "Skeptic," is the realization that you will always be biased and because of that you can train yourself to take steps to reduce the effects of your bias. If you convince yourself you aren't biased and a "Skeptic" as an endpoint and not a journey, then you will very easily fool your own mind and in some cases easier than someone who hasn't studied skepticism. Otherwise anything that seems right to you will sway you and you may end up falling for more falsehoods just like you may have as a theist.

Sadly, so many atheists are viewed now as know-it-all assholes who don't actually know that much, as they feel they got one question right on the test of life and think they aced the test entirely.

The Widow and the Mustard Seeds

A widow had a son whom she loved more than life itself who died suddenly. The child was her whole life and hope and her only reason for living. She refused to let them take his body away to the crematorium and held and hugged the child non-stop hoping that somehow their close contact would cause him to start breathing again. She was ready to give everything including her own life. Nothing anyone would say would make her give up. Then someone suggested that they take her to see Gautama Siddhartha. He just happens to be in the village. This appealed to her, as she knew he was a holy man and maybe he had some magical powers to revive him. If he was half as amazing as people said he was, bringing breath back into her son should be easy.

She went weeping and laid her son's body at the Buddha's feet. She said "You are a great master and know the secrets of life and death. I have come with great hope, please make my child live again."

He slowly and hesitantly replied, "I will do this, but only if you meet a condition I request first."

"I am willing to do anything for my son, even giving my own life," she responded passionately.

"Oh, nothing so extreme as that," he responded. "My condition is that you go around the village and bring me back a few mustard seeds from a house where death has never happened."

Parable of the Mustard seeds

So, in blind emotion she started her quest, going from house to house pleading for mustard seeds as if they were going to be used in a magical potion to bring back her dead child.

But at every single house, people with great sympathy said, "We can give you all the mustard seed you could want, but they won't help you. This house has not only seen death but thousands of deaths over the generations."

Every single household dearly wanted to help her but not a single one fit the bill. If anything, they were the opposite, and all had thousands of deaths occur in their households. By the evening she had a sobering awakening and came back a completely different woman. She was not the hopeful person who believed the rules of nature would bend to her. She was not special or different because her loss was any worse or her son more special than any other. She had become absolutely aware that death was a reality of life and cannot be changed.

"And what is the point? Even if my child lives a few more years, he will die again. In the first place it is impossible, in the second place it is pointless."

When she returned, she was very serene. She had asked the impossible. She dropped the desire. She came and fell at the Buddha's feet.

He asked, "Where are the mustard seeds? I have been waiting all day."

She laughed with gallows humor. "You played a good joke! Forget about it. What is gone is gone, sadly. Now I have come to be initiated to become a sannyasin (a nun). The way you have found truth that never

52

dies, I also want to find it. I am no longer concerned with bringing my child back. He is gone and nothing I can do will bring him back. My concern is to find the truth that never dies, the truth that is life itself."

Buddha responded, "Forgive me for asking you for something I knew was impossible, but it was a simple device you needed to bring you out of your own mind, and thankfully it worked."

The widow suffered from among other biases, subjective validation, also referred to as a form of truthiness made famous by Comedy Central satire host Stephen Colbert. It is a perception that is true if one's beliefs demand it to be. This bias can also easily link connections between coincidences leading to conspiracist thinking.

The Social Biases

As an individual, the other two types of biases are complicated enough, add the fact that we are a social species and suddenly it adds a whole new dimension to bias.

Another example of social bias is our **stereotyping**, expecting a member of a group to have certain characteristics without having actual information about that individual. It's a bias against things we are less familiar with and more trusting of things we know. Pop psychology loves oxytocin. It is considered the cuddle drug, but it's actually also at the very heart of racism and abusive relationships. When we have a high level of oxytocin, we are more trusting and altruistic of people in our ingroup. This becomes **Ingroup bias**, which leads to us being more judgmental, less altruistic, and less trusting of people in our outgroup. It's why a person who is infatuated with someone who you know is bad for them will view you as the enemy if you dare kill their oxytocin buzz by suggesting their current love is really not a very good person. You are now the outgroup and they are naturally prejudiced against you.

Sadly the only way to get them out of this situation is to let their heart get broken or for the infatuation to wear off and be loving and supportive and to be there for them and not have an I-told-you-so attitude or you could induce a **backfire effect** which is a bias where the brain, when presented with new information, will believe the opposite even more strongly.

Racism, bigotry and xenophobia is also hardwired and takes cognitive tricks to overcome it. In an MRI study, when a monkey saw a snake or a leopard, a part of their brain lit up as a threat. When they saw a monkey that was not in their ingroup, the same area lit up. When they saw a member of their ingroup, that area shut off. The exact same thing happened when they tested humans the same way. A brief flicker in most people was shown in the same areas as the monkey's brains, but our prefrontal cortex could override that and calm that area of the brain..

I even struggle with this bias. Growing up out in the middle of rural Indiana, I didn't come across many people who couldn't speak English. There, poor English skills were often either a sign of proud anti-intellectualism or poor intelligence. I moved to the city where a lot of foreign people live. So, when I hear them struggle with English, my brain naturally drops their IQ levels by a few points, even though I know logically that they already have a leg up on most people, as they know two languages and may sound incredibly intelligent in their own language.

BF Skinner, a behavioral psychologist, found that when he put pigeons in boxes and gave a button a clear pattern to

give them food, the pigeon, through trial and error, would find the pattern. If he made no pattern and what they did was completely random as to when they got food, they would find patterns that weren't there and do little rituals in hopes that the food would come because brains are natural pattern seekers, often even if there is no pattern. It is one of the major differences between modern computers and the human brain and what deep learning is trying to overcome. While IBM a few years ago did create a computer that emulated a single neuron, it will take decades to get small enough to reach the same density as that of the human brain.

Deep learning does it all the hard way by seeing something thousands or millions of times and then learning the best outcome, generating multiple random algorithms and keeping only the best ones and then altering and mutating it millions of times until they have one that is near perfect at finding that pattern. This is something we don't have the luxury of doing, but luckily our brains don't need to do this.

Because of this, our pattern seeker runs on a gradient, sometimes acting too strongly where there is no pattern and sometimes ignoring a pattern that is actually there. It is never perfect and will sometimes over perform and sometimes completely miss patterns, like an over- or under-sensitive smoke detector, sometimes going crazy when there is no fire and sometimes utterly

silent in a burning blaze.

Groupthink occurs within a group of people, because they desire harmony or conformity for the group. Being a group and collaborating can be very beneficial and is often the only way to do some projects. But if harmony and conformity are more important than truth and people in the group don't have the skills to get their egos out of the way for the sake of the project, it leads to an irrational or dysfunctional decision-making outcome. Group members try to minimize conflict by actively suppressing dissenting viewpoints, and by isolating themselves from outside influences. This can lead to judgements that are not even remotely true but if enough other biases are involved, it lead to disastrous consequences.

The Monk and the Prostitute

Buddhist monks would travel and beg for 8 months of the year and then stay in a house for 4 months during the rainy season. In ancient India, certain prostitutes were fairly high status. If a woman was considered a high enough level of beauty, it was considered unfair for one man to have her. So, she would take many lovers, including the local rulers, who would in turn lavish her with gifts and a way of life.

One day a prostitute named Amrapali looked down and saw a young monk and immediately became infatuated with him. He was a man with tremendous presence, awareness, and grace. He walked with nothing but the yellow robe and a begging bowl.

Amrapali immediately ran down and told the monk, "Please, accept my food today."

Around ten thousand monks were said to follow the Buddha to each town. When they found out that the young monk was invited in by Amrapali to her palace, they

felt their own egos under attack and jealousy filled them. Their strong desire was still too powerful in themselves.

After dining, Amrapali told the monk, "The rainy season starts in 3 days. Please stay in my house for the rainy season."

The monk responded, "I will ask my master. If he allows me, I will come."

When he left Amrapali's, a crowd of monks asked him what had happened, and he plainly told them what had transpired. Immediately, the shock of it all echoed through the crowds and word spread all over. Many monks told the Buddha beforehand to not let this happen. It must stop! It was a mix of religious dogma and jealousy and felt like an attack on them that they weren't chosen by someone so beautiful.

The Buddha responded, "Be quiet, all of you. He has not said he will stay. He will only ask me to stay. Let him first come to me and then I will decide."

The monk finally came forward and asked his master what had been requested by Amrapali. The Buddha looked into his eyes and said, "Yes, you may."

Of course, many in the community were shocked and furious. Ten Thousand monks were there. Why did this one monk get special treatment and they did not? They just knew he was going to spend the entire time not in meditation but giving into his lustful desires.

There was great silence.

After 3 days the young man left to stay with Amrapali, and after that there was nothing but gossip among the ranks.

"The whole town is agog. The talk of the town is that a Buddhist monk is staying with Amrapali for 4 months during the rainy season."

The Buddha said, "You should keep silent. 4 months will pass, and I trust my monk. I have looked into his eyes. There was no desire. If I had said 'no,' he would have not felt anything, so I said 'yes.' I trust him, his awareness, and his meditation. Why are you so agitated? If his meditation and devotion is deep, he will change her. If not, she will change him. It is now a battle between meditation and biological attraction. I believe he will come through this fire unscathed. Just wait 4 months. I have seen what he is capable of."

His followers would repeat the argument of, "The Master is too trusting. The man is too young, fresh, and inexperienced, and she is much too beautiful. This is an unnecessary risk."

After 4 months, the monk came and presented himself to his master. And following behind him was Amrapali, dressed now as a Buddhist nun.

"I tried my best to seduce your monk, but in the end he seduced me. He convinced me by his presence and awareness that real life is at your feet. I am giving all of my possessions to the commune of you and your

monks."

It was a beautiful garden and a palace, a space where ten thousand monks could spend their rainy season.

The Buddha then asked the assembly, "So, are you now satisfied or not?"

It was awareness that showed these monks their own deeply held biases and just how far they still had to go to be rid of them.

These monks collectively with their Groupthink, suffered from Illusory superiority where they will overestimate their own positive qualities and underestimate others. The Buddha had to go against their overwhelming groupthink and ignore them to decide on the best past and show them they were being biased.

Memory Biases

Biased memory is a family of biases such as the phenomena that one can easily forget evidence that goes against something they believe but remember evidence more easily that they like. This is related to the fact that stress helps us remember things better in the short term, but low stress and positive connotations are needed to help us remember things long term. Quite often in a debate a person can be convinced of a piece of evidence and hold it in their mind during the debate. They may plan to do further research on it to find out if it is true. You expect when you see them again to stop using one of their arguments that you pointed out and had convinced them to be flawed, but when you talk to them again and they have had time to sleep on it, they may have completely forgotten that your argument was so convincing. Many times, because they have figured out new ways to rationalize it away. I have seen creationists like Ray Comfort do this constantly. People pin him down and explain to him and convince him that an argument is completely flawed and needs to be thrown in the trash and the very next debate he uses the exact same argument with even more confidence that he is correct.

Golden Age Syndrome we discussed in the section on Buddhism is an example of the F**ading Affect bias** where you forget negative memories faster than positive ones. From it people infer that the past was always better and the world is getting worse, even if the data shows the exact opposite.

The **need for closure** is an interesting powerful psychological desire, explaining how the brain needs to feel like it knows, case closed. Ambiguity is too uncomfortable for the person. An interesting phenomenon in the human brain is called the **primacy effect**, where a person will make a positive or negative judgment based on certain descriptors or words. Studies have shown that if the brain cannot be certain, it will instead make a decision early on and later disregard new information. If the descriptors or experience of a person started out positive and later became negative, people would rate the person as better.

However, if the experience was reversed with the positives near the end, the people would list the person as less favorable. It's sort of the parochial effect but with judgment of people. The brain is usually too quick to make a judgment about someone without giving themselves the time to learn about the full scope of the person.

Stress of all kinds tends to increase the power of this effect, which is why one might make some really logical sounding decisions when tired or under stress, only to have it fail miserably. In hindsight, one will look back on the situation and realize it was a bad idea and be completely confused as to why they thought it was such a good idea at the time. The need for closure is so defined as a human trait that one can be tested fairly accurately on the "need for closure scale developed by Donna Webster." People who score high need closure and will be much more biased by the primacy effect. People who score low are just fine with having a more agnostic view of reality and can make much better nuanced decisions.(Webster, 1994)

Easy answers are everywhere in the world we live, while finding the actual truth and hearing both sides of the story requires work and effort. So many jump at the first explanation they hear and freeze any new information from registering in their brain.

All new information is rejected even when it completely and rationally destroys the person's original belief or if new ideas they accept completely contradict their original ideas. They will believe both without question or face scary uncertainty. It requires a person to train themselves to deal with uncertainty and be ok with not knowing to overcome this natural bias and lower their need for closure score.

Countering biases

The best way to counter biases is self-awareness. Buddhism has many stories of people overcoming a particular bias about a particular subject using mindfulness. However, they did not have science and psychology to help them target biases overall. Roughly a third of all biases known to psychology could be countered if more people understood psychology as they would be able to question their own memory and stop ourselves from going with our gut feeling about our identity and another third could be easily countered if they understood how statistics worked. The Gambling industry that relies purely on luck such as casinos and the lottery is driven entirely by people's lack of awareness of their own limited mind's inability to grasp emotional manipulation and that we are inherently bad at understanding statistics.

There are some things our brains are naturally good at, language being one of them. If you take two kids who have never heard a spoken word and isolate them, they will come out speaking a brand-new language with most if not all of the parts of speech we have. Twin language or cryptophasia, a naturally occurring language shared and created between many twins, is a good example of this trait(Thomas, 1996).

Unlike language, Math, reading, writing, methodological science and

your brain. I would always tell my students that boredom was actually them getting smarter and if they pushed through it, it would increase their capacity for knowledge further down the road just like healthy muscle fatigue and soreness will increase your muscle capacity.

Scams and addictive gambling, especially with modern computerized slot machines, rely on people's biases and limits of their brain at every turn. Magicians do too, but they are generally not scamming you. They are telling you up front that they are lying to you. With good training and education in psychology and statistics, we would only have to focus on the final third poison and Buddhism mindfulness would help counter that.

However, there are groups, especially on the internet, who refer to themselves as Skeptics. I do not call myself a skeptic, as being a systematic skeptic is not a destination but a journey. A path one can follow that will take one's entire life and you will still have unexplored biases you never knew you had. We will always be plagued with biases, but we can get closer to the truth by learning tricks to counter them and hold off our desire and need to believe something immediately.

When I see a new science study, the first thing I do is drop it in the "maybe" category. This is exactly what scientists want you to do but not what the brain evolved to want

systematic skepticism are all counter-intuitive to the way our brains evolved. They only arose in specific areas of the world, most often to deal with some problem that hunter/gatherers never had such as calculating taxes or inheritance. As the need for the skill arose we became capable of grasping them by taking unrelated parts of our brain and strengthening their connections purely through practice so the brain was capable of doing superhuman feats. Boredom is like soreness or tiredness in your muscles for to do.

It's why the news, especially in the US – because it is looking for a sensational story – will take a scientific study and couch it in terms of certainty. A study that says, "There is some evidence that in this particular situation for this particular disease, eggs may be beneficial but more research is needed," becomes "Eggs are good for you!" once the media gets a hold of it.

When a study offers, "Possible negative correlation in regards to a particular situation for a particular disease, in certain cases eggs may be harmful, and more research needed" becomes, "Eggs will kill you!"

This seesaw of science reporting of oversimplified complex data from just reading the abstract is why so many people think that scientists don't know what the hell they are talking about. They're just guessing! It turns out it's not the scientists, it's the news that doesn't know what they are talking about. But news often doesn't want to bother to hire actual scientists to write articles with understanding of nuance and it's not flashy and, frankly, pretty boring. It's why NPR and BBC are much better at reporting science than news that relies on ratings to survive.

The entire list of logical fallacies can easily be looked up on Wikipedia. You can take them one at a time and work on them piecemeal or you can get the general idea and find the patterns and work on them all

together. This is not something you can do overnight. One's mind can't deal with that much change, but it is something one can work at little by little until they have created new pathways to get around certain biases.

The Diamond and the Lotus Flower

One morning Great King Prasenjita, at the behest of his wife, came to Gautama. She had been going to see and listen to him any time he was in town until she got married. She had told her husband, "You waste your time with idiots, talking about unnecessary things. Gautama Buddha is in

61

town, go see him!"

He had no interest, but after enough insistence he finally said, "I guess it is worth at least one visit to go and see what kind of man he is."

He was a man of great ego, so he did not want to go as an ordinary man. If he was going to go, he wanted all the Buddha's attention. So, he took out his most precious diamond to present to the Buddha.

He wanted everyone in the crowd to know, "Who is greater, Gautama Siddhartha or King Prasenjita?" He was so great that he could hand over a diamond that wars had been fought over as if it were nothing.

His wife laughed at him and said, "You have no idea about the man I admire, you would be better off taking a flower than a rock." He was confused, but as there was no harm, he took the most beautiful lotus flower from his pond with him as well.

When he reached the Buddha, he offered first his diamond in one hand. The Buddha looked uninterested, though clearly

knowing its value simply responded, "drop it."

Very surprised, the king dropped the diamond that wars had been fought over and people had died for. His wife may have been right, so he instead presented the flower. As he tried to offer the lotus to the Buddha with his other hand, the Buddha responded yet again, "drop it."

And so, he did.

He stood there, worried that the man was insane, but there were ten thousand disciples sitting around him worried about what they must think of him.

Buddha spoke a third time and said, "Didn't you hear me? I said drop it."

"   Was he crazy?" The King thought, "I dropped the diamond, I dropped the flower, I don't have anything left to drop."

At that moment, Sariputta, an old disciple, started laughing. Mortified, the Great King Prasenjita turned toward him and asked like a deer in the headlights, "Why are you laughing?"

"You don't understand the language

he is using. He wasn't saying to drop the diamond or the lotus. He is telling you to drop yourself. Drop your ego. You can have the diamond and the lotus back, but leave your ego and don't take it back with you."

The ego is one of the biggest barriers to truth. To overcome it takes a lot of work and is a constant journey and it constantly gets in the way. There are methods to overcome it, using and practicing tools called systemic Skepticism or just Skepticism, although many confuse it with the colloquial definition of just disbelieving everything or things they don't want to believe, which invariably makes them feel smarter. But, of course, this is not the truth.

Carl Sagan

While Carl Sagan did not invent systemic Skepticism, he was one of the most prolific figures to popularize it and worked with others to create rules to help one increase their own skepticism.

It is part of the "Baloney" detection kit one can learn and perfect to prevent being taken advantage of but also be able to avoid being cynical and a "curmudgeon," as Sagan put it, distrusting everything and everyone. When you have a good baloney detection kit, you can not only eliminate what is false but it opens up the path for what is true and who you can trust most of the time, although even then you must keep a little healthy doubt of them in mind. Perfecting these rules takes a lot of practice and humility but when you have achieved them it will be much harder to be taken advantage of.

He was a strong advocate for spreading scientific knowledge and awareness in his day, something the average scientist kind of looked down on and beneath him at the time as the cold war had ensured they would always have enough funding. It was only after the cold war ended that they suddenly began to realize that they needed the public to be knowledgeable enough to ensure they kept funding and didn't start outright rejecting science and following harmful claims.

How to be a good skeptic and prevent bias

Be prepared. If you are going to try to argue and you didn't do any or enough research into a topic then you just brought your knife to a gun fight and you will lose.

Here are two lists of rules to be more

Detective Bragnir always follows the evidence

skeptical, laid out by CSICOP, The Committee for Skeptical Inquiry of the Claims of the Paranormal, an organization founded in part by Carl Sagan to counter bogus claims being made in his day. One discusses personal skepticism to keep in mind at all times, and the other is how best to debate anything with someone else from a skeptical and honest angle. Since then, they have been reworked. There are several versions out there you can find online including one list by Michael Shermer.

Rules for Personal skepticism

-Follow the evidence:

Just like a detective follows clues, these clues when properly assessed are called evidence. One has to be careful not to contaminate the evidence. If one is able to solve the case, the evidence will be used to convict the person and send them to jail. If the evidence gets contaminated or is no longer usable, then the criminal might get released because there is no evidence of his crime, or it could send the wrong person to jail. We live in a system where, supposedly, people are innocent until proven guilty most of the time otherwise we would send a lot more innocent people to jail. So we cannot make any positive assertions until we have enough evidence. Science uses the same principle. It collects evidence and analyzes that evidence. Every new idea is assumed false until proven

64

true by sufficient evidence.

Sometimes the scientist will make evidence via experiments, and everyone can learn how to make this evidence and repeat it. Sometimes, like in a crime case, the evidence can only be found, and they have to use science and past cases to discover what happened.

-Remain open to new discoveries:

If a detective has a case and one thinks that a person is guilty, one will think that the person is guilty because she has enough evidence. If a new piece of evidence is discovered or one finds out one of their pieces of evidence was wrong, one may have to change their mind about the person they thought was guilty.   It's difficult and means that one may have to come up with a brand new suspect or might just find out that the person did it but did it differently than one first thought. One may have

enough evidence now or they may have to go look for more evidence.

-Take a cautious position until the facts are in:

Innocent until proven guilty. If someone tells you something, try not to assume that what the person is telling you is either true or false unless you have enough information to make a good decision. If you just assume what you want to believe based on what you think about the idea or the person, you will probably make a bad decision.

-Always do the math:

Make sure that your math is correct. If you are using statistics or mathematical figures that don't add up it will lead you to the wrong conclusion and hurt how people see you.

-Be prepared to change your mind in light of new evidence:

Many times it is really hard to change your mind even when you can see the evidence for yourself. You want to believe you are right. Feeling wrong can make you feel stupid. But feeling bad won't help you be right later. Everyone has had to change their mind when presented with better evidence. Do not feel dumb, mistakes and errors in knowledge are how learning begins.

-Be respectful when challenging ideas and beliefs:

Being arrogant, a know-it-all or a jerk won't help anyone, and others will be less open to changing their mind.

-Read! Always keep reading.

Reading is important to being skeptical and being right. Things we know change as new discoveries occur, so if you stop reading you may fall behind in your topic and end up being wrong. Also if you are skeptical of a broad topic, not reading enough may make you miss some major evidence that will make you come to a wrong conclusion without it.

Once, it is said, lord Buddha took some dry leaves in his hand and asked his favourite disciple, Ananda, to tell him whether there are any other leaves besides those in his hand.

Ananda replied "The leaves of autumn are falling on all the sides and there are more of them that can be numbered." Then said the Buddha "In like manner I have given you a handful of truths, but besides these, there are thousands of other truths more than that can be numbered."

-Always fact-check, even on positions you agree with:

This is the most difficult thing for a person to do, as looking up references and citing sources takes time and energy but I can tell you that many times there was something I was sure I knew was right but after looking into the research I had to admit I was wrong about what I thought I agreed with. It is humbling but that is part of being skeptical. Even in writing this book there were a few things I had learned in the past that when I looked them up, it turned out I had either heard wrong, remembered wrong or the source had been wrong. And there are probably even a few things here that are still wrong even after having people who know the subject matter look over it.

-Be aware of your own biases.

Biases are what happens when you want to believe something, or you believe something without question. You need to be aware of these or you end up getting bad information in your studies. Scientists have tests called controls to prevent their own biases from getting in the way.

Sariputta was a Brahmin that came with his 500 disciples to debate the Buddha. All were great scholars.

The Buddha welcomed them warmly and said "I have heard your name. I must ask, have you experienced the truth or are you just a great scholar?"

Sariputta hesitated, looking at the Buddha, fully exposed and said, "I am a great scholar, but as far as knowing the truth for certain, I have not known it"

Buddha said "Well that makes arguing very difficult. Argument occurs between two people who don't know the truth. They can argue until eternity playing with words and logic and quotations and scriptures but there is no possibility of coming to a conclusion. At best the more cunning and tricky person may defeat the other in semantics or sway the crowd with better showmanship, but is this any way to decide the truth?"

"Or there is the possibility of two people who know the truth and then there is nothing to argue about. They will be in the same space and be silent."

"There is the third situation where one knows and one does not. Then that is troublesome because it is hard for the person who knows to translate what he does know into the language of the ignorant one. The one who does not know will be unknowingly wasting his time and mind because nothing in the world will change the mind of the one who knows."

"You have come with your 500 disciples. You don't know and are certain that none of your disciples know either, or they would not be your disciples, they would be your master. You are older and more scholarly than they. How are we going to discuss anything? I am ready... but I know. One thing is certain, because you do not know, you cannot convert me. The only possibility is you will be converted so think twice, and even then we may both be wasting our time"

But Sariputta was already converted. The man who had defeated many great scholars in debate. It was a requirement by the scholarly mob to be considered a wise man.

"If you are really interested in the truth, and not in getting defeated or victorious, as that is not my interest, I am here."

Sariputta replied "I know that I can neither argue now nor be able to argue later. You have finished my argumentation. I can't argue because I don't have eyes, and when I do have eyes we will agree." so he and his five hundred disciples joined and followed the Buddha.

He said to his disciples "I am no longer your master, Here is the man I will follow. Please forget me as a master, if you want to be here, he is your master now."

Many people seek knowledge not as a way to be better and smarter but to be better and smarter than you. They debate and pwn (internet slang for owning/beating you) and use showmanship to win debates even if they aren't really correct. This makes for a great lawyer but a terrible seeker of truth. Now the Buddha mentioned experiencing truth, but direct experience as we know thanks to biases can often not be true, and we now have science to help us discover truth. However this "need to win" instead of the need to actually have two people find the truth is a problem that has plagued us for thousands of years, even before the internet came about.

Rules for discussion and debate

-Clarify Your Objectives.

You must make very clear your reasons as to why you disagree and what points of their argument you feel are wrong, otherwise you will just make stupid arguments and look like an idiot

-Do Your Homework:

Do not go into a discussion unprepared, make sure you know all angles and sides possible. If someone disagrees with you, find out their reasons first, they may have evidence you are completely unaware of. Then go research their evidence.

-Do Not Go Beyond Your Level Of Competence:

Only argue the areas you are trained in. Do not try to argue with a quantum physicist if you did not study the same amount in the same field. If one is trained, they can do meta-studies which all people in science should be able to do. Meta-studies are using the analysis of works and papers to create a collaborative study, but they still have to have it checked out by someone of a higher education in the field before what is being said has merit. People of cross fields can look at paper or claim and find out if it is bogus, but they can't make new claims to replace it without asking experts to verify them. I would have to say the only area this is not true is politics because we are all technically capable of and required to choose someone to vote for. Even if we aren't experts in the field, we have to try our best to discover the truth, especially if we have a cause we care about.

-Let The Facts Speak For Themselves.

Only present facts and evidence, do not try to interpret them to fit your needs. It may get you in trouble if you overstep the facts and they will require more facts and evidence from you to back up your claim

-Be Precise:

Speak clearly and don't get off topic or jump to a different discussion point if you don't like where the discussion is headed, especially if the subject has you looking in the wrong. This is what a skilled showman debater does but doesn't get anyone closer to the truth. Also try to eliminate extra facts that have nothing to do with the topic, otherwise you will confuse and bore people with whom you are discussing the issue.

-Use The Principle Of Charity:

The principle of charity is the assumption that the person you are debating is not lying to you. Many people will do this and assume that the reason why they think differently is because they are evil. Assume that the person with an opinion is not actually bad, just misinformed and completely honest about what they think. Also, make sure to assume that you too could be wrong. Not knowing the other side's point of view makes you just as bad as they are even if you believe your position is morally superior. Your moral superiority could actually be false if you don't charitably understand why they believe as they do.

-Avoid Loaded Words And Sensationalism:

Some words affect the way people react emotionally. Sometimes you can cause people to agree with you, even if you are wrong, because you are using their emotions against them.

Neither of you learned anything and now you both will believe a lie and possibly convince other people of the lie. Lies are bad because the only way to fix a problem is to know the truth. Also, if you spread a lie and people find out that it is wrong, they won't trust you later on when you are telling the truth. Be aware that other people may try to use charged words to play with your emotions and try to convince you this way.

They may try something like this: "If you don't believe me, we could all die!" This argument may be true, but if there isn't enough evidence to back it up then the person is using fear to try to convince you. "We'll I guess you don't really love your child." This is trying to use guilt to make

you agree with them. It doesn't make them right. Anger, reward and other emotions are used by people to convince you that they are right. It doesn't make them right; it just makes you and them feel a certain way. The evidence doesn't care how you feel, it's the evidence.

Overcoming your own biases requires you to not take anything personally. Any attack on your ideas must be separated from your personal identity, your ego. If they are rejected by the authorities of knowledge on that subject, they aren't insulting you, even if they appear mean about it. It means you haven't supplied sufficient evidence. If a person rejects your idea that is 100% true, it doesn't mean you are wrong, what it means is you aren't explaining it well enough, or

that person isn't ready to change their mind that fast, as paradigm shifts are rough.

Gautama Buddha went to a town and a crowd surrounded him. They yelled, jeered, called him every vile insult they could think of. These were conservative Brahmin Hindus and he dared to speak out or against parts of the Vedas, their holy scriptures. He called the priesthood parasites and exploiters, similar to what Jesus had said about the Pharisees and Sadducees. The Buddha listened silently, without showing a hint of anger or rage. His disciples on the other hand were getting furious. How dare they mock their great and wise master? But since the Buddha didn't act, neither did they. He just stood there, acting like they were telling him some interesting idea or even praise.

After a certain point of listening he finally said "If you have said everything you want to say to me, I would like to move on to the next village where people are waiting for me. But if you are not finished, I will come back in a few days and I will let you know I am coming so I can finish hearing all you have to tell me. Thank you."

One in the crowd shouted, "Are you stupid? We aren't telling you anything, we are condemning you, you ex-Brahmin, you heretic! How dumb can you be if you are just standing there instead of realizing we are attacking you? You should be furious!"
He chuckled a little bit at that and shook his head.

72

"I'm sorry, you have come a little too late for that. If you had come to me to tell me these things ten years ago, when I was as blind and insane as you are, not a single person in this village would still be alive tomorrow. I was a prince and warrior then and considered by some a great swordsman, assuming that too wasn't a lie created by those ordered around me by my father. You Brahmin are all thinkers and not fighters and I could have massacred you then easily. But thankfully for you I am no longer insane. I cannot react. But I would like to ask you all one question. In the last village people brought me gifts: fruits, flowers and sweets. However, we only take food and just enough to live on once a day. And we had already eaten that day. I told them we are sorry; we cannot take your gifts. We accept your love, but you will have to keep those. I have to ask you all what do you think they should have done with the gifts, sweet food and flowers they gave us?"

One replied, "Obviously they should have distributed them back to the village."

"Well that is very sad," He replied "I cannot accept what you have brought for me, what will you do with what you brought to give me? If I don't accept them, your insults, your condemnation, your offensive words, what are you going to do with these words? Take this abusive garbage and distribute it to your friends? Your family? The vulnerable? You will have to distribute it because I refuse to take it. And you cannot make me angry

unless I accept your insults, unless I take what you are giving.

"Ten years ago, I was not awake. If someone insulted me, I would have taken that person's life or lost my own to challenge my honor. At that time, I did not know that insulting me is his problem, not mine, and I have nothing to do with his problem. I can only listen to his problems compassionately and then walk away"

They weren't attacking him; they were insulting his ideas. He was not his ideas and their insults weren't arguments or teachings but ad hominem attacks that lead neither of them further to the truth. So, he just listened and moved on.

This is a great lesson to learn for dealing with internet comments.

How to Tell if Someone Is a Pseudo-scientist

1. They try to disprove or make claims beyond the scope of their field or specialty (Ex. William Dembski is a mathematician trying to argue against evolution and genetics, something way beyond his scope of knowledge.)

2. Books and not peer reviewed papers are published

Any schmuck with a laptop and an idea can publish a book. It requires the ability to have your evidence stand up against the rigors of peer review that all ideas have to go through. Lay people don't have enough information on the topic, but they will eat it up if you present it in a logical but ill-informed manner. This is not to say that there are not the occasional amateur scientist that is published, It is very rare but it has to make it through peer review which is made up of people who spent their life studying that specific field.

3. Claiming persecution by the scientific community

If your theory holds value, weight and evidence on an issue, just like in court, no matter how crazy and unlikely the idea is, it will win in the end. Whining about persecution to the layperson is a PR stunt, a smear tactic and no more. It does not give your idea any more credence to stand on. If a scientist's idea is not accepted to begin with, he or she will adjust their controls, and go back to doing more research so that they can prove it better or find out they were actually wrong all along. All peer review feels mean, it sucks to put something through peer review. Take it personally and you are going to hate your life no different than if you were on trial and the prosecutor felt mean. Vilification is useful for the gullible, but emotions and facts like to disagree a lot.

4. Use of private and fake "peer review journals"

It sounds sciency so it must be true. These are attempts by people who could not get their ideas published in a real journal. To appear legit, they publish a "peer review" journal aka a fake journal with all the trappings but with other people agreeing with everything the other person writes. In a real journal the burden of proof is on you and every dot and cross is scrutinized in case you had an error about something. The massively embarrassing errors known to the scientific community that make it through fake "peer review", are staggering. All of these are used by creationists, cryptozoologists, alien visitation proponents,climate change deniers, Qanon believers, Intelligent Design proponents, anti-vaxxers, many alternative medicine practitioners, and paranormal proponents.

Part 3: Buddhism the Religion

"The teachings of Buddha are eternal, but even then Buddha did not proclaim them to be infallible.

The religion of Buddha has the capacity to change according to times, a quality which no other religion can claim to have...

Now what is the basis of Buddhism?

If you study carefully, you will see that Buddhism is based on reason.

There is an element of flexibility inherent in it, which is not found in any other religion."

- Bhimrao Ramji Ambedkar, The Buddha and His Dhamma: A Critical Edition

Buddha's death

The Buddha had a practice in his old age of dining with the first person who came to him in the morning. This never meant poor people, as the wealthy had the ability to wait and not work to be the first while the poor were too busy trying not to starve. In this case, the king was on his way but his Chariot broke down. The king was delayed by a few minutes and by the time he made it, Gautama had already accepted the invitation of a poor man. It makes me think he should have picked a more equitable system of picking people, but I digress.

The King said, "I recognize this man. He is Cunda the blacksmith. He has tried for years every time you come to visit. He has nothing to offer. Please reject the idea of going to his house."

"That is impossible, I cannot reject an invitation I have already agreed to, even if the king asks," The Buddha replied.

So, he went. In Bihar, the place he was staying at the time, poor folks picked mushrooms and dried them to eat during the rainy season. This man only had mushrooms and rice to offer. The Buddha ate the food just as graciously as if he was dining with the king. The mushrooms were bitter but because he desired nothing, he was not disappointed with the mushrooms being bitter. He gratefully thanked the man for his meal and then left. The next day he died.

One of the last things asked of him was "Why did you go? The king warned you. You are 82 and need the right nutrition.

"It was impossible. When the truth is invited, it must be accepted. And he invited me with such love and passion, an amount no one has ever shown me in my life, that it was worth risking my meager life."

The next morning, as he lay dying, he said, "The last day has come and my boat has arrived. And I must leave. The journey with all of you has been wonderful. I could not have asked for a more beautiful life thanks to all of you. If you have any questions to ask, I will answer them, as I will not be physically available to you soon."

Everyone was crying or sitting in stunned silence. No one had the energy to speak or ask. The Buddha almost certainly laughed in pain and said, "Don't be sad. This is what I have been teaching you all this time. Everything that has a beginning ends, even me, and I will not be ending, only our time together. As I have taught you with my life, let me teach you with my death."

People were teary-eyed as they watched him. "Well then if there are no more questions, I will be off." Laying on his right side with his head in his hand, his last words were, "Be a light to yourself." He passed the responsibility to the person to find their own way to enlightenment.

According to the Mahayana, Gautama died on Parinirvana Day sometime in February, while the Theravedans and Vajrayans say he died on Vesak, the day he was born, so that he reached enlightenment and died all on the same day of the year adding to its auspiciousness, and, subsequently, suspiciousness that it's not even remotely accurate.

This is one of many versions of the Buddha's death. It is murky and there are 3 sources with conflicting writing, one of them being compiled very late and the most accurate account containing two different accounts of his death. The most trusted being Maha Parinibbana Sutta from the Pali collection of the Digha Nikaya. It paints two differing narratives and personalities. Along with the one just discussed there was another narrative about how the Buddha saw a vision that he was going to die. However he discovered he had the ability to remain on Earth as a god, but only if he was invited to stay. However Ananda failed to invite him, so he left this plane. It is believed this is a coded commentary about a political conflict at the time and not meant to be taken literally.

There are variations even in what he died from or how he died. The Theravedans put the meal he ate as being sukara maddava or "Pigs Delight," a pork-based meal, while the Mahayanas claim it was just the rice and mushrooms, possibly because of their belief in vegetarianism.

There is even debate about his final cause of death. Was it spoiled meat or rice? Was it the poisoned mushrooms? Some say

that when presented with the meal he asked to only be served the food and for Cunda to bury the rest, knowing it was too rotten or poisonous to eat. My first story I heard from The Guru made it sound like the Buddha knew but ate it out of kindness as it would hurt Cunda's feelings. I always found this horrifying as to how narrow-minded to refuse food knowing it would kill you out of kindness but without taking into account just how devastated Cunda would have been knowing that he killed the man he most admired.

The Buddha instructed Ananda to assure Cunda that it was not his fault, it was something else, which may be true, as while some say it was rancid pork growing Clostridium perfringens or poisoned mushrooms that killed him, some scholars think from the description it was actually a

mesenteric infarction, a symptom of old age, rather than food poisoning. They can't even agree if he died at 80 or 82.

That being said, much like Gautama Siddartha's life, his death was also lost in a tangle of myths. The truth as we see it will forever be obscured in the many truths of the narratives used at many different times in history to help convey his message. Be a light to yourself. Find the way to your own enlightenment. Don't rely on him for it or you will never find it.

Buddhism as a Religion

Buddhism is a child of Hinduism, so it's naturally messy to pin down. Is it a religion or is it a philosophy? Victorian era Europeans really had problems defining it. The answer for most is both. There were schools of Hindu philosophy that were very much

79

religion where emptiness and poverty were viewed as good things. No self, no thing, no unaware action, no conflict. Under Emperor Ashoka who ruled most of modern India and Pakistan around 250 BCE, Buddhism grew by leaps and bounds supported by the government. This increased its ability to be communicated to others but it also became more political, and wealth was pumped into grand shrines and monasteries, kind of defeating the purpose.

It began to focus more on doing culturally viewed good things and less on focusing on removal of one's attachment to this world to attain Nirvana. Merchants on the Silk Road would bring back their riches and commission beautiful art and statues, including the great Buddha statues in Afghanistan that the Taliban blew up. This was to build their karma by spending their wealth, which also bought them social capital and stroked their own ego, as opposed to dropping their ego and giving everything away and living as simply as possible in obscurity like what the core of Buddhism said was needed to attain enlightenment and to escape Samsara.

During the middle ages, Christian monks had this same problem, where they would live as humbly and poorly as possible and knights who slaughtered tons of people would pay these monks to pray for them to forgive their sins using their pillaged blood money. The poorer the monastery, the

atheistic, and there are ones who believe in many gods and some who believe that all those gods are an aspect of one god so great our mind can only process in the tools of 33 million gods and personalities. Add even more complications when Buddhism leaves a Hindu-heavy India and moves into another country to complement their local beliefs and religions.

Buddhism began in northern India near Nepal. From there it branched out into many Asian nations, often fusing into the other religions.

In India it started out as a form of

higher in demand these monks would be as their prayers were believed to wipe out more sin faster. Then they became rich and powerful and corrupted by wealth, buying up land from under people and became viewed as tyrants, exactly the opposite of what they set out to be.

In their westward expansion, the Buddhists used the Greek language to spread their message, as Alexander the Great had conquered much of the lands. After Alexander died, local kings representing the former Grecian Empire converted to Buddhism under the control of the Mauryan Emperor Ashoka who had converted to Buddhism. It would have been interesting if Buddhist missionaries had made it all the way to Greece and Rome and gained a foothold in Greek philosophy at the time, as the world now would be very different. However, that did not happen for various reasons.

Buddhism spread to Sri Lanka with the Theravada school with a very similar flavor, as they were heavily influenced by Hinduism. The island is still 70% Buddhist and 12% Hindu.
There was an incursion of the Muslim Mughal empire and an absorption of the

Buddha into the Hindu religion as an avatar of the Brahama. This was followed by the takeover of India by the British empire, which brought in many Christian missionaries to India. Buddhism's birthplace over time became made up of more Christians and Sikhs than Buddhists. Sikhism was viewed by some as a hybrid of Islam and Buddhism, since actual Buddhists now make up 0.7% of the population of India, while Christmas make up 2.3% and Sikhs make up 1.7%. So, at this point the link between Buddhism and India is torn aside. When we think of Buddhism now, we tend to think further East and North.

It later moved to southeast Asia, all the way from Myanmar to coastal Vietnam, blending with the local religions and traditions. Theravada, called the little boat, was the much more secluded version of Buddhism, where often the most elite monks cloistered themselves away from the average person, and one gained status in society by being a temporary monk and it merged with what the locals currently believed. Any culture with ancestor worship or belief that a dead human could become a god would have no problem praying to and deifying the Buddha like any other god. Each culture blended the Buddha into their own pantheon of gods, sometimes replacing the head god and sometimes as a special side god, untouchable and powerful but not caught up in the affairs of gods because he was above it

all being enlightened now. In some cultures, he was a creator and a destroyer, in some he ruled over the dead or decided how they would reincarnate. In some he was a Jesus figure ruling over heaven and letting good people in and comforting them.

The movement along the silk road to Han China occurred in the first or second century CE. The third century was the first record of the translation of Buddhist texts from Sanskrit and Pali, to Han Chinese. The difference between China and India could not be starker in how they viewed religion and philosophy. We will go into much more detail and reiterate this discussion in the second half of the book, but while Buddhism gained a foothold in China, it wasn't without some compromise and controversy.

At the time, the two major schools of thought that almost acted more like political parties were Confucianism and Taoism. When one was in favor by a king, the other was either diminished in patronage or outright persecuted. It cycled through the generations and when Buddhism came in, it fared no differently. Buddhism disagreed with both Confucianism and Taoism as they both viewed reincarnation as a bizarre concept and death was final, but especially so in Taoism as immortality was attainable and worth seeking. What was here in the real world was what mattered more than after death. Confucianism was about strict discipline and cultural and tradition norms

and roles. Taoism and Buddhism were always about questioning norms. Taoism as a religion also involved ancestor worship and some shamanistic and animistic beliefs.

If you wanted to compare the 3 to modern US political parties you could jokingly refer to Confucists as Republicans who didn't mind a lot of big government and big government spending, Taoists as a hybrid of Libertarians and the Green Party, idealizing nature and self- dependence, and Buddhists as modern Democrats who weren't really big on democracy.

The Mahayana branch, called the big boat, predominates in China and believes that one can find enlightenment by helping others find enlightenment. Unlike in southern Asia, where they often isolated themselves from the common people, Buddhist

monks were much more approachable and helpful in their practices and many picked up Taoist beliefs and ideas in the process. Exorcisms in Buddhism became a normal thing and invoking the name of Buddha could have a similar impact on spirit possession as invoking the name of Jesus in the West.

In Korea and Japan, Animism and Shamanism were the main beliefs. Buddhism was not seen to interfere and cause major problems with their religions, so it was allowed to prosper. Japanese Shinto even found it to be a useful companion as it addressed aspects of life and added rituals that Shinto lacked. Buddhists in Korea did have a period of oppression by neo-Confucianism but when Buddhist monks rose up to rebel against the Japanese invasions of the 1500's,

the persecution of Buddhism stopped and it began to rise in prominence.

Zen or The Ch'an School

In Zen Buddhism, the masters like to have paintings of the Buddha around, though depicted ridiculously and out of proportion unlike the Indian depictions of the Buddha. The serious sacred Buddha is distorted, made silly and even mocked in depictions in Zen. The fat Buddha is believed by some to be one of them, he has a belly because without it he can't have a true belly laugh.

The Zen Master Bankei always insisted on having a painted image of the Buddha hanging behind him and he would say, "Look at this fellow. Whenever you meet him, kill him immediately. Don't give him a chance. While meditating he will come to disturb you. Whenever you see his face in meditation, just kill him then and there, otherwise he will follow you and haunt you, If you repeat his name," he would say, because Buddhists often chant Namo Buddhaya, namo buddhaya, "immediately go wash your mouth out with soap." But then his followers would see him bowing to the picture every morning. His followers were confused and Bankei replied, "All of this has been taught by this fellow, so I must pay my respects."

This is insulting to the Buddha on purpose. Laugh at him, make fun of him, there is nothing special about him. It is an act of love. The second you have an image of the

Buddha in your mind, you place your own interpretations and biases on him. When you say his name, you do so as well. When you think about a fact or the Truth, you do the same. Even the great Buddha could, *gasp*, be wrong! Have no preconceived notions. In the pursuit of truth, nothing is sacred.

When the Buddha debated, some monks were more in tune with him because they understood the logical battle. When he spoke, others understood the words and their meaning, but when he sat there silent in front of those two groups, it felt awkward and uncomfortable. But not the monk Mahakashyapa.

Mahakshyap felt most at ease and in tune with the Buddha when he was silent. He felt such wisdom in the silence, and the limits of talking. The Buddha just sat there holding a flower, silent. But the other two groups were all restless, wishing this was over, so they could finish up and go home. Mahakashyap found this so funny, and he laughed out loud. Everyone else was utterly appalled that he would do so in front of the great master. It's irreligious, profane and disrespectful. However, in Zen, laughter is a tool, like the fat buddha is displaying. A chant, prayer and mantra.

The Buddha looked out on the crowd and called him up. He gave him a flower and said, "I give you the keys. What are the keys? Laughter and silence, silence within, laughter without. And when laughter comes out of silence, it is not of this world, it is divine."

Or, as I like to say, "Blasphemy with an equal mix of humility leads to enlightenment."

Because of this, Mahakahyap is considered the first master of Zen Buddhism. Sadly, often people think blasphemy alone makes them superior or humility alone makes them righteous and neither ever sees the truth.

The Ch'an School of Buddhism was an interesting marriage of Taoism and Buddhism.

The first practitioners of Buddhism in China were Taoists. They adopted the meditation techniques of Buddhism and blended it in with their own meditation practices such as

85

qigong, a form of mindful moving like yoga that is believed to help with the flow of energy or qi and used in martial arts cultivation.

In China there are 3 different masters, each a master of a part of Buddhism. There is a master of rules and discipline for monks and nuns, a master of meditation, and a master of the writings of Buddhism. Different centers focused on different parts of Buddhism.

Ch'an believes that all sentient things have enlightenment but our experiential and social training has covered and cluttered that up so we can't see it. It is why animals appear to be always in the moment while we are always planning for the future or thinking about the past.

This idea of a natural state is very Taoist. It involved accepting past transgression of both others upon you and mistakes you made in the past as things that happened and accepting them in a non-judgemental way. A modern interpretation may be that because we were developing and didn't know things at the time, there is no way to judge our past selves, only our present self for not learning from our mistakes and what we know now and make amends for our past actions, not out of guilt but out of knowing more and growing.

We are also driven by emotions, bad psychological mechanisms and chemical imbalances that shade our judgment. As we grow and gain awareness, we are less controlled by our mind's drugs and we gain psychological tools to control our own nature. We are the sum of our experiences and memories, and the more memories and experiences we have, the more we change as a person, if we can learn from our behavior and correct our ways of thinking. The Ch'an believe that the sutras, while a useful introduction to Buddhism, are useless compared with thoughtful interaction with the world.

Ch'an also says we must accept our circumstances at this point in time. If we have good fortune, it is fleeting, so do not be too happy about it or that will just lead to suffering when the good times inevitably go away and the emotional high crashes. Give up all craving and desire to eliminate suffering and focus on the right actions and thoughts.

They also believed that enlightenment could come suddenly to people sometimes out of shock, though most often gradual. Hence, in Zazen temples, when the Ch'an moved to Japan, Buddhist priests would and still will hit you painfully with a stick if you can't meditate in a group to correct posture and to shock someone out of being lost in mental verbalization and imagination to break them free from concepts. This can in their thinking sometimes shock you into enlightenment or epiphany like how a blow to the head in movies cures amnesia.

There may be something to this method of thinking. Blaise Pascal said that "All of humanity's problems stem from man's inability to sit quietly in a room alone." The human mind hates the lack of stimulus.

A study was done where people prior to the study were given a painful shock and asked if they would pay money not to get shocked again, to which most said yes. They were required to sit in a room alone for 15 minutes with no stimulation. They were given the option to push a button to receive a shock if they wished, to which most participants laughed. Over the course of the experiment it turns out, boredom and mental stillness is less preferable to any stimulus, even a painful one. Some shocked themselves every 30 seconds just so something was happening even if it was negative(Wilson, 2014).

It is said that the opposite of love is not hate but apathy, as you get no attention at all.

When I used to get acupuncture, after doing so I felt like a Zen master. The type I used required attaching a TENS unit or electrified pulsed low current to the needles

87

while forcing me to lie there and not move for 15 minutes to a half hour. If I didn't relax, the pulses would hurt and become unbearable, but there was always some stimulus. Over time, thinking I was doing good things for myself, I began feeling pretty proud of how strong a current I could take and not feel it. Because I felt so amazing afterwards, I believed strongly that Acupuncture really did have powerful properties.

Science says otherwise, but this type of acupuncture did have positive advantages. Not because it was doing anything medically to me, but because it was forcing me to relax and essentially meditate on the pulses. It gave me the option of a shock if my brain got bored and it eased me into being able to sit without any other stimulus and enjoy it. However, you may be able to get the same benefit from a TENS unit without needles, and it would cost you a tiny fraction of an acupuncture session which can run you

$50-100 a session. If this is what the Zen are accomplishing, then there is some science to back them up.

Ch'an or Zen also were big on the idea of Koens or poems given from the master to the student to meditate on and find the meaning to it—assuming there was any meaning from it that could be put into words. Some were meant to be nonsense to break one out of their own stuck way of thinking, some were about observations of the little things in reality to increase mindfulness, and some were there to contemplate the wholeness of reality linking enlightenment with the Chinese concepts of Wuwei or the Tao. When the koens became too literalistic, some Buddhist monks would burn them because the koens were now ruined. Zen, along with Tibetan Buddhism, are probably the most known forms of Buddhism in the West.   Zen appears to be the most packaged version as a philosophy with the least baggage of religion. It has a lot of merits like other forms of Buddhism. It's much stronger in Japan and Korea, although we can see it was somewhat absorbed by the Jingtu or "Pure land" Buddhism in China.

Jingtu or Pure land and Shin Buddhism

Pure land Buddhism is a departure from other forms of Mahayana Buddhism and takes on almost a salvation religion aspect akin to Christianity as opposed to a way to change one's own mind to allow for a free mind. They believe anyone can achieve nirvana by chanting and performing rituals.

A century later, a branch of pure land Buddhism was invented called the Shin sect. They believe anyone can gain enlightenment more by their faith in the Buddha and less about what they do or how they think about reality and attachment. A belief in and prayer to the Buddha will allow you to naturally have the "right thinking" needed to gain enlightenment. While there is more nuance to it, a complete history of the topic would complicate this book much more than the points I am attempting to get across as it has become divorced from the core philosophy.

Tantric Buddhism

What is Tantra?

When people think of Tantra or Sutras, they usually think of Tantric Sex and the Kama Sutra. It sticks in their minds because of the sexual implications. However, the word tantra and sutra means to weave or warp. The defining of a tantric belief practice of religion is a mostly Western idea and a concept created as a way to make sense of other ideas in eastern thought. It is viewed more as an esoteric or mystery and ritual driven belief system similar to alchemy, Christian theosophy, or the kabbalah. The belief that practices and rituals can uncover mysteries of reality.

Another difference from most forms of Orthodox Hinduism, Buddhism and Jainism, a tantric Buddhist can reach enlightenment by being successful in the world. They can find parts of enlightenment littered throughout any experience in the world. To them monasticism can be a self-delusion to enlightenment and can limit your experience of reality.

Very early Tantric traditions arose in Hinduism and included yoga and holding complex poses to gain spiritual enlightenment. This may have evolved from similar sexual tantric practices as part of a fertility or sexual worship branch of Hinduism. Tantrics also do not shun or fear death. They may live in or near a cemetery and smear cremation ashes of their lover or friends on themselves to contemplate death as a natural part of life. Skull men figures or kapalikas exist in both Hindu and Buddhist tantric traditions, where the practice of tapping the skull will help determine when the person will be born in the next life.

Tantric Buddhism has spread throughout Asia from India and Pakistan and heavily merged with and influenced the Bon religion of Tibet. As Tantra is a created term by the West, it's not exactly set in stone what practices define it, but here are some common themes:

"Skull cup (Kapala)"

-They center around ritual, especially in deity worship, mantras and mandalas, to name a few

-They visualize and identify with a deity, as in, to take on traits of said deity

-There is a need for initiation and an importance of having a teacher or guru

-They will engage in anti-moral acts that break down societal norms such as use of sex to attain enlightenment

-Re-evaluation of the body, such as removing connotation from the parts being dirty or clean, or sexual and non-sexual

-Re-evaluating the status and role of women as, in tantra, women hold a lot of enlightenment knowledge and are viewed as equals in tantra and have control in ritual sex and their orgasm is more important and sacred than a man's

-Analogical thinking or finding meaning of the macrocosm in the microcosm of say a mandala painting or simpler systems

-Reevaluation of negative mental states, such as lust, anger, fear, greed and so on

In Tantra "negative" mental states are a natural part of us and to attempt to deny them from existing just makes you a slave to the opposite instead of true freedom. In Buddhist Tantra, engaging and allowing traditionally negative mental states can allow for a middle path of acceptance instead of just avoiding them. Tantra, in its traditional form, requires the cooperation of a wise woman, to balance the two types of energy. Without the balance you can't have Tantra.

Tantrics use many techniques or sadhana to gain spiritual power or in the case of Buddhists, enlightenment. They include: gifts to their guru, initiation rituals where a guru may transmit spiritual energy to you, yoga, mudras or hand gestures, mantras, mandalas, Yantras or symbolic diagrams of universal forces, hymns, deity self-identification, ritual sacrifice, use of taboo substances such as drugs, nyassa or touching parts of the body while reciting mantras, ritual purification, puja or ritual worship, an explanation ritual if the puja is performed wrong, guru devotion, pilgrimage, vows such as fasting, abstaining and using Siddhi or supernatural powers, ritual dancing, ritual feasts where a meal is offered to deities, ritual sex and dream yoga or lucid dreaming.

While starting out in Hinduism, branches of Tantric Buddhism evolved, Vajrayana being the most popular one, Tibetan Buddhism is a form of Vajrayana Buddhism.

Origins of Tantra in Hinduism

In Hindu Tantra, the goddess Shakti and the god Shiva represent energy and consciousness, which also represent what was used and created during conception

when a new consciousness is formed. A spark of bliss during love making mixed with the generative fluids of male and female plus energy and consciousness from the partners created a brand new consciousness and that bliss stays with the person all their lives. Consciousness that can experience the universe, and they can go on.

God is viewed as part of everything and everyone; recognizing the god and goddess in oneself is essential. Shakti is the creative force to make and destroy, and has many avatars including: Mohini - the Temptress, Lakshmi - the maternal principle, Saraswati - the creative aspect, Kali- destruction. One could easily include every single other female deity from any other culture as God is made up of 33 million avatars of Hinduism.

Kali is depicted as a maniacal violent goddess wearing a necklace of human skulls. She is depicted dancing on the corpse of her lover, Shiva. Shiva is often described as her footstool or mattress, and when not dancing on him, she is mounting his phallus, which is the only thing that animates his corpse.

This symbolizes that without each other, pure energy runs amok, and consciousness is dead. When in perfect harmony, new life is created. Female energy is the raw energy, and male energy is more like a computer of consciousness that is 100% useless without electricity to power it: literally, a corpse

At the Temples of Khajuraho and Konark in India, there are Tantric Temples. No other temples are like these. The exterior of the temple is covered in carvings and reliefs of every known sex act imaginable and many that are physically impossible to engage in. They are meant to shock and be profane the most puritanical believers who view sex as base and immoral. As you go inside, the carvings get fewer and fewer. The sex begins to decline the further you go into the Temple. Couples carved deeply in love, looking into each other's eyes, holding hands smiling and embracing but no sex.

Going deeper in the adornment becomes less and less. In the innermost part of the temple, the Gharba or womb of the temple, there are no figures, or lights. It is silent, empty and calm. The Gharba is meditation, samadhi, within oneself. The exterior is sexuality and noise and revelry. If you repress the exterior you destroy the interior. They are part of the same continuum. Tantra is neither blind hedonism or sexuality, nor is it blind reverence or spirituality. It is both. Doing one with awareness and mindfulness empowers the other.

The profane is just natural

Until you can accept the profane as also a part of nature, you can't begin to understand and accept the beauty of reality. I forget daily as a microbiologist that discussing diseases in depth is usually not consid-

ered polite conversation or table talk, but without my and my field's acceptance and normalizing of them in all of their horrendous disgust, we wouldn't have either the knowledge needed to cure people of them, or the mental fortitude necessary to do the "gross" work necessary required to study the body and disease at its very core.

As a child, I couldn't imagine doing what a nurse does, cleaning bedpans, stabbing people with needles, cleaning up blood, wiping patient's most dirty parts. Yet these people are heroes and do this every day with little thanks. They got over the gross factor that we were all raised with to help people get better or at least live with some measure of dignity on their way out. They deal with death daily, so we don't have to think about it that much.

Most of these disgusts, which we all have, are good during our childhood and adolescent years. Playing with fecal matter isn't exactly the best idea, and a mix of nurture and nature disgusts us to protect us from catching diseases. The same is true with many body fluids. Transmission of disease is so easy that if you don't have the knowledge to protect yourself to handle these potentially dangerous substances with the respect and reverence they deserve, you could get very ill. It is quite interesting that people in poorer nations with less easy access to good healthcare and sanitation have a naturally

worse disgust factor to most things, especially fecal matter. Their risk is much higher, so disgust is a self-preservation mechanism, but when the risk is lessened and you still respond with the same level of disgust or fear, that is a rather unhealthy phobia that can impact the rest of your life(Skolnick, 2013).

As someone who has a disgust factor to the thought of same sex couplings, it is that disgust factor that makes me completely understanding of people only wanting members of the same sex and finding no attraction or even being disgusted by doing sexual things with the opposite sex. However for the longest time, people couldn't get over the gross mental image of two dudes going at it, instead of focusing on it as a natural

part of reality and a way to express love, or just a way to have fun and bond in your own way. I feel like people overshare about their fetishes these days, but I'm glad there are spaces where people can share and trade safety tips and feel safe to discuss things that the majority would find messed up or disgusting.

A gun deserves respect, but one can enjoy firing it with the right training and precautions. With the right training, awareness, safety engineering, respect and regulations, one can reduce all accidents to near zero. Without these, you are playing with a time bomb that might go off at any time.

A wild animal is the same way. If you have methods to train or protect yourself from being attacked and know what you are doing, you can work with wild animals. Constant mindful awareness and respect is essential, and if you take any of it for granted even for an instant, you could end up maimed or dead. These experts have this practiced so well it looks like they are being careless, or wreckless because it's become second nature and they can do it within a window of safety and never go beyond that, similar to how I can deal with biosafety lab level 2 pathogens without thinking about it. They know what they are doing inside and out. I deal with both contamination of samples and infectious agents. I have to respect both my ability to infect my samples from my body and methods that I can get infected

from those samples. I have them down pat, so much so that I have not had contamination from standard procedures (knock on wood) in the 15 years that I've been working in the field.

In America we have abstinence only and many of us grew up with D.A.R.E. and were taught that all sex before marriage or drugs were bad. You are a chewed peice of gum if you have sex with multiple people, not to mention all to the diseases a filthy slut can aquire. So don't do it. The same with drugs. You will always end up a meth head in the gutter if you smoke one joint, or drink

alcohol depending on the level of religious purity you were raised in.

For me, visiting Europe was a shocking change in life. People did lesser drugs without thinking about it but did so respecting the power of the substance. The same is true with sex. Nudity is normalized there. It's fun, and it's not scandalous at all. They focus on violence as being an issue. In Europe, US PG-13 violence gives the movie their equivalent of an American R rating. But turn on the TV and depending on the country, you can see full frontal nudity during daytime and prime time hours, things that would make American mothers clutch their pearls saying "Think of the children!"

Sex to many in Europe is just a natural fun thing. In Germany, you often don't confess your love for quite a while after being together and sexually active. Sex is a thing that you are told all or most of the dangers of in sex ed class, and then taught how to take precautions so that the risks of a negative side effect are that of driving a car. Girls start off on birth control early, Contraception is easy to access, testing is available and promoted thanks to universal healthcare and because of universal healthcare, Abortions tend to be restricted several weeks earlier than even in US as they have the tools needed for an early abortion before the zygote has developed.

Weed, and hallucinogenic mushrooms are legal in the Netherlands and movies stereotype the Netherlands as being full of hippie potheads, but the Dutch actually use weed at half the rate Americans do because it's boring and they have never had a death from hallucinogens. America made it taboo, Netherlands did the opposite. The only hallucinogen related deaths are from tourists who don't treat the drug with respect ingrained into them and they go do something stupid that a Dutch person never would.

Now that pot is legal in many states, that weed culture I grew up with is rapidly dying. You are seeing a spike in usage this generation but I will bet that you will begin to see a decline in the next generation because it's boring and just, ok. DARE taught us that weed was on the same par with hard drugs, and was a gateway drug making it taboo and some studies show that DARE may well have increased illegal drug use in kids once they promoted it as the forbidden apple you should never partake and on the day you eat it you will surely die.

Abstinence-only classes in Texas spiked the number of teenage pregnancies (Stanger-Hill & Hall, 2011), Free IUDs and birth control from the state of Colorado tanked them. Sex is going to happen. It is a fact of life. Meeting reality where it is and people where they are instead of where you judgmentally think they should be can save lives, reduce abortion rates, and unwanted, unready single mothers (Cherry, 2017).

In much of Europe they are taught how to enjoy these vices and still be safe, in America, especially in the religious community, we are just taught, DON'T. Just don't. I have seen straight edge teens turn into alcoholic sex fiends over night once the genie comes out of the bottle. They were never taught how to approach these things like an adult, like an engineer, to be safe and treat it with respect. It was a taboo, and an evil thing to do and once one has engaged in one evil, one might as well go all out and ask for forgiveness later leading to some very dangerous side effects. Addiction, accidents,

STDS, all that could have been prevented with some training on how to do things safely instead of keeping them in the dark about that and just saying don't eat that apple.

What is very interesting is that the generations most likely to be against sex ed are much more likely to engage in unsafe sex or sex in general than the generation they are raising.

Thanks to good sex ed, impulse control and cost benefit analysis along with lack of boredom for stimulation in the modern era, Teens now are having way less sex than their parents and grandparents ever did and their parents and grand parents are having unsafe sex on a mass scale to the point that STDs ravage retirement communities(Smith, 2020). The adults were never taught to be adults about sex so they villify it and treat

it as evil to their kids yet then do the exact opposite themselves. They need sex ed worse than their kids do.

Their kids on average realize all of the risks and complexities sex can bring. Some are foregoing it until later because that is a whole can of worms they think would complicate their already stressful school and social life. Some are engaging in it safely. Others, such as ones raised religiously are finding loopholes to losing their virginity from everything but full on intercourse thinking they are being safe when they are actually in some cases being more dangerous.

That is essentially the core idea and point of tantra. Awareness, safety, knowledge, and destroying taboos that are 100% natural, instead of the very a puritanical mindset of just don't do it that leads to never growing up about it and fearing the natural needlessly. Not having sex to not complicate your life is just as Tantric as having lots of tantric sex. It's not done or avoided out of fear or guilt, it's being done with full awareness and safety.

At the tantric temples, the faces are all blissful, at peace, meditative. Outsiders may only look at the genitals and the sex, not at the faces, contemplating, happy and at peace. They aren't obsessed with sex, and they aren't afraid or ashamed of it. They are living in the moment fullying enjoying it full of mindfulness and meditation. They are playful, having fun, not taking it or themselves too seriously. If it's not playful (unless that is your fetish), it's just a motion you are going through to meet a need you were denying. It is similar to drinking and eating. If you aren't taking the time to enjoy it, and putting variety and experimenting with it, you are just mindlessly consuming, which can lead to obesity, or denying a natural stress reducer. It is the middle path. Fear and disgust are addictions to one mind drug/emotion, obsessions and hedonism are addictions to the opposite extreme.

Sleep is natural. Too much or too little are not good, just enough is just right. During the industrial revolution as lights were invented, sleep was considered a luxury not a necessity and only the lazy slept a lot.

This mindset progressed up until just recently and we are finding that too little sleep leads to wasted time being awake because you have to go back and correct the mistakes you made. You are angry and irritable, making enjoyment of life much worse and you are more prone to depression and addiction. Getting the right amount is hard work, and everyone needs varying amounts, some based on genes, some based on age, some based on lifestyle. But we all need sleep, just not too much of it, and being obsessed with sleep is also neither healthy nor productive.

The power to be serious and sober minded at some times and the power to be able to play at others, this adult/child duality is essential to a healthy life. The Buddha meditates but he also laughs. He sees reality for what it is not for what he thinks it should be and accepts that before he can even pretend to begin to change that reality, or he will be disappointed and suffer.

The Founding of Tantric Buddhism

The founder of Tantric Buddhism, Saraha, has a similar story to that of the Buddha and written to be a little too perfect, making one question its basis in reality. The story is set up to add legitimacy to the movement including the idea that his master was trained by the Buddha's son. Saraha which means "he who has shot the arrow" was originally named Rahula, and he was the best of his brothers. His father was a wealthy Braman and the king thought Saraha was the bee's knees so much so that he tried to persuade him away from becoming a Buddhist monk, including giving him his daughter and marrying into the royal family. But he resisted all these ideas and left to study under his new master.

After renouncing wealth, his Master told him he had to renounce what he thought he knew about the Vedas or Hindu texts and scriptures. Renouncing wealth is one thing, renouncing knowledge is another. It is part of one's entire identity to be "smart" or "learned." Many people often only gain knowledge not so they can be better and smarter for anyone's benefit but so they can lord it over others. Knowledge is a tool that should be used for the purest of reasons and

giving that up is a huge and difficult part of giving up one's own ego.

From then on, Saraha became a master of meditation, and people came to look upon him meditating. Here was a very attractive man with innocence that of a child during his meditation. One day, while Saraha was meditating, he was said to have had a vision of a woman in the marketplace who was to be his real teacher and his current master, Sri Kirti, had only set him on the path. His way to enlightenment was not for Saraha.

The marketplace is the opposite of say an ashram. Ashrams are quiet, solitary, contemplative, reflective. The marketplace is loud, packed with people, and reactive. While alone your brain can self-analyze. While surrounded, your brain doesn't have the processing power to do that, so it can only react. So far, the Buddhist tradition had been male dominated, but his master sent him off with his blessing, laughing, and told to find his new master. Saraha went to the marketplace and did in fact find the woman from his vision. She was an arrowsmith, both mature and wise.

An arrowsmith woman is of a low caste, according to Hinduism. The higher born and cultured and civilized you are, the less likely you are to have a tantric transformation because you are programmed with pomp and circumstance and superficial pageantry, political wrangling and manners, while a person from a low caste ignores all of that. They don't have time for that. They are too busy getting by on street smarts and how they can get enough food to eat to survive. People of both worlds learn entirely different skill sets. It is one of the reasons why it's difficult for both classes to understand each other. Rich people are really bad at understanding why poverty exists and poor people couldn't even begin to understand the insanely byzantine world of the rich with wealth displays and power politics.

Being uncivilized, uncultured, and uneducated are highly important in Tantra. The learned, powerful and cultured going to the uneducated, powerless and uncultured is symbolic as both sides are required to attain tantra. So, Saraha saw this woman, alive and radiant, blocking out all the noise and distractions, focusing solely on cutting an arrow shaft and making an arrow. His old master had focused on a philosophy of anti-philosophy, which ironically is still a philosophy. This woman had no philosophy. She didn't have time for that kind of contemplation. She was more about living and reacting, not about thinking. The powerful unchecked energy of Shakti to his completely refined, controlled and cultured Shiva.

As Saraha watched, she took the arrow, closing one eye and focused on an invisible target standing in the pose of an archer, completely lost in the action of testing the arrow out in her mind and seeing how it

would fly and if it was good enough to hit its target with a competent marksman.

In many stories this woman is actually a Dakini in disguise, or a sacred female spirit. Being that the story shows this woman knew things about Saraha that she wouldn't probably know under normal circumstances helps lend to this narrative. He was said to have asked her if she was a professional arrowsmith, and she just laughed a wild laugh.

"You stupid Brahmin! You left the Vedas but are now worshiping the Buddha's sayings instead. You just pointlessly changed the books you followed, and you are still just a stupid man."

No one had ever talked to him with that raw, unchecked honesty that would in any civilized society be viewed as rudeness. In some circumstances, that could possibly lead to legal repercussions or even death. She was so uncivilized, so primitive, that it drew him to her.

"So, you think you are a Buddhist hmmm?" He looked down at his yellow robes, a bit shocked. "Buddha's meaning can only be found through action, not words or books. You have wasted enough of your time trying that. Follow me and I will show you how to find the truth through action."

Her focus on her arrow neither to the left or the right suddenly revealed to him how the true middle of meditation and Buddhism is meant to be, action and meditation, reflection and reaction. Without action, meditation is just a pointless exercise. She could both meditate on the arrow and focus solely on it, while acting to make it. There is a reason why people love crafts, they can focus completely on it, lose themselves in it, and see a thing they created through their actions. It is much more satisfying than most other work.

In the past, artisans just did this. They worked on the same product from start to finish. But with mechanization, and supply lines forcing people to do the same repetitive step over and over again rarely seeing a finished product, Marx's idea of worker alienation came into play creating a worker as Adam Smith put it "as stupid as one can become." Arts and crafts or building of any kind is a form of meditation, and it has payoff. One must learn to be prepared for setbacks and not be disappointed and give up when there is an accident, or something doesn't go right. One has to be able to adjust to find the point that is just right in the middle.

Saraha had moved from the dogma of the philosophy of the Hindu Vedas to the dogma of anti-philosophy of the Buddhist texts. She was neither. In the middle. She was too busy acting. Do something completely and the memory of it fades, the door on it closes. This is the **Zeiganick effect** we discussed back in the section on the Biases If you start one task but get redirected to another task, you can't fully focus on that task. Your memory hangs open and uses energy to keep that tab on your mental browser open. It's why psychologists consider most versions of multi-tasking a myth. Trying to do more than one thing at once bogs down the mind. It is why people with ADHD multitask as their brain is moving a thousand miles an hour and they get bored so easily, so they need the mind to slow down a bit. However, once addicted to multitasking, they can bog down their minds so much they can't function or end up making mistakes even though it used to work well for them (Hallowell, 2011).

The need for closure is also one of the reasons why people would rather accept a wrong answer than a simple "We don't know yet" from science. Crafting allows you to focus, create, complete, use, and forget.

All the things the brain craves, all of the things tantric action is about, losing yourself in short term memory of the now, the past and future don't exist, only the now. Doing things completely or not at all and knowing which ones you will complete and which ones you won't or learning to do so in a very healthy manner where you learn to accept incompletion and imperfection is tantra.

As the poet Paul Valery wrote, "A work is never truly completed… but abandoned." Knowing at what point is good enough for you to be done is essential to being good at any task, and is the same mastery a scientist has to have over the "need for closure" of going as far as they can on a subject and stopping when they reach the end of what can be known at the time. They

have abandoned the subject but like any craft it is as close to completion as anything can ever be.

"I apologize, you are not a mere arowsmith. I am sorry that I ever thought of you as ordinary at all. You are a great master and I am reborn through you. I was not a real Buddhist until today, I was not a real Brahmin until today. You are my master and my mother, and I am reborn through you."

She accepted him as her disciple, and they moved to a cremation ground to live together. They lived in the cremation grounds to be near death, to not fear it but to contemplate it right in their faces and accept it. They became lovers with both physical and mental intercourse, mutual meditation and learning exchange.

Saraha stopped meditating. Singing, dancing and lovemaking at a cremation ground, a place of death and mourning were now his mediation. He became aware and mindful of all he was doing, but also losing himself in the awareness of the moment. It was the joining of the opposites into a continuum and realizing they are both part of the same reality, sadness and happiness, male and female, birth, sex, and death. We just happen to be at certain points depending on where we are in time, and often those points are split through self or socially imposed denial of the other part of the continuum.

He was playful, no longer serious. He was capable of being both but had spent most of his life serious, he needed to relearn the playful to be able to be in the middle, or each extreme when the need arose. Just as people used to come to watch him seriously meditate, they came to watch him sing and dance in ecstasy, and began engaging in it themselves, infectious to those around and the cremation grounds became a place of celebration, turning the opposites on their heads.

Of course, the Brahmin, the puritans, the conservatives hated him. He was overthrowing their reality, their emotionally held ideals, triggered their disgust factor and in some cases threatened to overthrow their power. They began proclaiming him a pervert, a fallen Brahmin, a false Brahmin, and Buddhist monk who gave up celibacy and indulged in shameful practices with a low caste woman. That his ecstasy, dancing and singing in a cremation ground made him look like a mad dog. He was just insane and had completely lost it. He was a mental health disaster.

The king began hearing about one of his favorite subjects going completely mentally unstable and began sending people to confront him. It is said that he sang 160 verses of a song to the doubters and they never returned without being changed and danced and sang as well. The Queen who loved him like a son and had desperately wanted him to marry her daughter went to go see him. She heard 80 verses and didn't come back. Finally, the king, who was both worried and confused, went to see Saraha in person. He heard 40 verses and began dancing like a mad man as well in the cemetery.

Saraha has 3 scriptures. The 160 verses are called the People's song of Saraha, the

G. PAULI (Sweden)   MIDSUMMER'S NIGHT

80 verse Queen's song of Saraha, and the 40 verse the Royal song of Saraha. He had to use more words with the people because he didn't speak in ways they could understand as well, or usually interpreted, because they were less learned and needed more instruction. The same is true with the queen and the king. He knew exactly how to communicate to the king his thoughts because they were both from the same background. He knew what the king knew and didn't know and all the nuanced wording that would make him understand. It's usually translated that he had to use more verses for the people because they were less knowledgeable, it is perhaps the opposite and he was just less knowledgeable of them and had to clarify more due to his lack of cultural understanding and nuance. It is an interesting formality and word usage.

In Japan, honorifics are everything. The first few minutes of any live tv show involves honorifics and ensuring everyone is properly introduced. In parts of China, families or close friends don't even say please or thank you. To western ears it sounds like a rude command, but to ask for things implies formality or fakery, the love and devotion is implied already by not having any honorifics or what others would view as manners. Saraha had a direct shortcut to how the king could absorb information.

It is said in the scriptures that once the king was converted, the nation was con- verted and "became empty", in the Buddhist sense, the nation became egoless, and at peace. Basically, the nation all gained enlightenment.

If only it was that easy.

The brain is set up to fear change, and resist it like a phobia. Paradigm shifts are rough because they take time to process. This story is myth for the most part but full of symbolism for understanding tantric Buddhism better.

Normalizing the profane

When a member of certain tantric sects joins, part of his training is to sit and look at a naked woman. Others might see this as a perverted act, especially in more puritanical practices. Instead it is created to normalize the lust driven taboos.

Clothes are an interesting phenomenon. Around the equator, most people go naked, the further away you get the more clothes and more layers of it you have to wear. Nudity becomes rarer and rarer and more sexually arousing, making it all the more dirty and sinful. Taboo is created through rarity and wanting more. That is not to say taboos don't exist around the equator. Many tribes may have a custom of a woman always covering her shoulders, or thighs, while the breasts and genitals are fully exposed. They don't view either as sexualized parts of the body. Any place that is covered and made to be taboo suddenly becomes

the object of desire and less a normal part of reality.

In tantra, one has to get over that lust, that guilt, that desire, and normalize the thing they desire. Once normalized, it no longer controls them. In certain studies, before pornography was easy to get ahold of, rapists given porn were less likely to rape. Rape is about power to take something they desire from someone else. With nudity becoming normalized, some stopped desiring that. For others, though, it was about taking what didn't belong to them and what others valued and continued. How that study translates into the modern world of internet porn and if that study was flawed, we may never know. For sexologists, it's nearly impossible to find a control group who have never looked at internet porn to find out.

When people heard about Saraha sitting in front of a naked woman, people would say, he's done what we all desire to do, but I've denied myself that desire, which makes me better than him. The difference is that nudity becomes normalized, whereas the effort to resist the desire in the first place instead of giving up that desire is more of a mental hindrance.

Action, sex, nudity, are all there not as the end goal, but a method to just be. Being is more important than all other things. Some reach it through meditation, some through monasticism, some have to learn to go to the opposite of what they have always

106

been to reach the middle like a folded piece of paper. It is about breaking out of the duality and becoming whole again. Words are not needed during sex especially at and after orgasm. They can very much get you to that point, creating arousal, and are essential for consensual sex, but at a certain point when both are present and in the moment, they aren't needed, and stop meaning anything. They are gibberish, fake; focusing on the moment and the experience is real.

That said, the end goal of sex isn't always orgasm. Often, it's for bonding. It has many uses. Even if you don't feel like it and achieve the end goal for a few sessions, laying down still helps with rest even if you don't sleep, meditation still helps even if you don't reach Zen. Relationship time still

creates bonding even if you don't "glow" emotionally after. It requires effort and action just like a person who is making something, doing things that take days or even weeks to reach fruition.

In the end though, to reach a state of tantra requires a complete state of trust and communication with the other person. Trust to be seen naked in both physical, emotional and mental senses, all of their oddities and flaws included, and see them as beautiful art. Playfulness can be very awkward when you start out. It requires building trust. At a certain point you may try to experiment, try something new, a new position, a phrase or gesture. The other partner has to be supportive if it gives their partner pleasure but not mock the other person because it's not their

cup of tea—they should make them aware that it doesn't do anything for them.

Playfulness is a game of trial and error and enjoying the process with glee. If you are given feedback without taking it personally, you can narrow in on what truly brings you together and if you fear to give feedback because it could cause hurt or anger, or if you fear to receive feedback and take it as a personal attack, it can't be playful. Nothing can and you may live under the delusion that you are the best lover ever because you can do a set of things even though you are just the best lover for one specific person or they are faking pleasure.

Many people will often learn how to please one woman and then when they break up will try to do the same things to their next lover. Everyone's nerves and brains are different. A man may try to do that thing that made the last woman orgasm like mad, and the next woman either doesn't like it or it does nothing for her. What makes a person a good lover is not the skill to do a specific sexual act, but to make the other feel at ease to give feedback, without fear of getting one's ego crushed or fear of crushing their ego.

Playfulness leads to relaxation. Without trust, safety and playfulness, relaxation is impossible, one is always on eggshells. One can't reach climax, or only does so with much difficulty. It is why many women have never reached climax, all of the social pressures preventing them from truly relaxing and enjoying what is going on. Will they anger the man? Will this make her a slut? Will people judge her? Will he judge her? Is she pretty enough? What about that blemish that advertising told her is utterly disgusting and makes her a swamp monster? Until both egos are dropped and made to feel like communication and exchange is free without obstacles and one can see the beauty in all things, tantra is impossible. Without trust tantra is impossible.

.

Tibetan Tantra

It is interesting to note that Tibetan Lamas consider Saraha their founder but also have taken vows of celibacy. Vajrayana is the third of the 3 major branches of

Buddhism and while there are many schools inside of it, all branches of Vajrayana contain some forms of tantra.

To some, Vajrayana Buddhism is just Mahayana Buddhism but with a quicker method added on to it, while others view it as superior or completely different to Mahayana. Members of both groups often view the Theravada Buddhist practice as inferior as the "little vehicle" or even translate it as "defective" and very difficult to gain enlightenment from, as its purpose is to gain only enlightenment for one's self and not about gaining enlightenment to spread it to all of reality.

The Theravedans on the other hand, view the idea of liberating everyone to reach enlightenment as a fool's errand and a dogma that is not at all possible. They can lead a horse to water but making them drink is another thing entirely.

Vajrayana Buddhism is called the diamond or the thunderbolt vehicle, relating to the mythical weapon, the Vajra, an indestructible weapon, the double-sided club with a ribbed spherical head, sometimes with a blade on each side. It was wielded by the god Indra, a storm deity, who's Vajra was formed from adamantite and could cut through anything. It is considered to be one of the most powerful weapons in the universe according to Hindus. Indra was an indo- aryan deity that appears to have come to India during the axial age along with a host of other deities when they immigrated to northern India in what appears to be a

one must empty themselves to attain enlightenment, and it also represents the void from which all creation sprang, while the clapper inside the bell symbolizes form and empathy.

Vajrayana Buddhism is believed to have spent much time during medieval India working alongside Shaivism or the esoteric worship of Shiva as wealthy people and royalty paid to have temples built that they both had to share causing them to trade ideas with each other. This pairing formed as early as 100 CE and is why in places such as Bali where Hinduism is the predominant religion, the Buddha is Shiva's younger brother and certain holidays such as the festival of silence, or Nyepi, are officiated by both Hindu and Buddhist priests.

Following this pairing from sometime between 300 to 1300 CE, a sect of long haired traveling monks supposedly from the Bengal region called Mahasiddhas traveled around and used many of the techniques Saraha is said to have used, living in crematorium grounds and engaging in left handed practices such as the taboos of ritual sex and ingestion of taboo substances, all the while mocking and challenging establishment Buddhism. Much of their formation occurred as an aggressive and defensive position against the medieval practices of using violence to force obedience by those with power who were deified, which establishment Buddhists at the time were complicit

mostly peaceful immigration. As the Indo-aryans branched out from the Iranian areas both east and northwest it is possible that Indra and Thor and even Yaweh could be versions of the same initial storm deity.

The most common Vajra, the five-pronged Vajra made up of 4 ribs and a central prong represents on one side the five poisons of the material or phenomenal world of samsara and on the other side, the five wisdoms of the noumenal world or Nirvana. It is considered the male piece often paired in meditation with the bell, which is the female aspect, associated with the wisdom of emptiness. This reminds them that in. Rumors of magical powers and abilities to control ghouls and other forms of spirits, as they lived around the dead, helped give them some level of protection in this era of persecution against unorthodox ideas.

In fact, many of these practices for much of tantric history were for the procurement of magical powers including weather control all the way back to the Vedic period or early hinduism. The very first tantric sutra, written in the 7th century CE called the Tattvasamgraha Tantra was the first to focus on using tantra for liberation

and enlightenment as opposed to being used for these powers.

Vajrayana practices differ from Mahayana in the fact that the Mahayana focus on taking their natural Buddhahood and cultivating and growing it like a fruit while Vajriyana views everyone as having a fully formed Buddha within them, they just need to learn to dissolve the ego that is currently drowning it out. After that they can focus on visualizing and internalizing the Buddha, the eternal Buddha or Amitabha, or any number of local deities as they all are aspects of the

greater Buddha.

As Vajriyana evolved this deity visualization, it began to replace much of the left handed acts of tantra, and instead they visualized tantric sex with a deity as a divine consort of perfect enlightenment, instead of actually practicing taboo acts in real life. This is why the Dali Lama is celibate even though he is technically a practitioner of tantric Buddhism and a follower of Sara-ha. Mantras and mandalas and all forms of mental visualizations have replaced much of the physical taboos of the old Mahasiddhas.

Another strong aspect of Vajrayana is the reliance on lineage of the guru tradition; a relationship between master and pupil. Tantra is viewed as esoteric and mystical by many, though some masters claim that it's not done purposely. It's just that, just like the Buddha telling one person there was a god and another there was no god, their teaching is tailored to the pupil as opposed to being tailored to all. So taken out of the context of the master-pupil dynamic the words and meanings are all lost because they weren't meant for you and you have very different needs, biases, and ignorance than the pupil the words were first said to.

While Vajrayana Buddhism spread far and wide throughout all of Asia, including to the Mongolian Khanates who made Vajriyana Buddhism their official court religion in China, and every Asian nation has a few schools in the tradition, it is mostly popular now in Tibet, Mongolia, Bhutan, and Nepal. In Nepal the monks do not practice celibacy unlike the Tibetan version.

However as Tibet becomes more culturally and ethnically cleansed by the Chinese Communist Party, Vajrayana may end up considered a minor school even in once heavy Vajrayana Tibet and perhaps shift its practice centers to Mongolia, Bhutan northern India or some of the Russian or former Soviet nations as they all have areas with high populations of Tibetan traditions of Vajrayana Buddhism.

So what is Tantric Buddhism?

Tantric Buddhsim is meant to be one of many methods to reach the middle way, by taking the extremes and tying them together and breaking down the taboo. Doing so with full awareness and control. To normalize the desire so the desire doesn't control you, to challenge and overcome the "ick factor" as a mental exercise so that something that is gross to you and the desire for it to go away doesn't control you and you can think about it without negative reactions getting in the way. It is one of many ways for a Buddhist to achieve the middle way and become whole. It is not just about sex, nor just about death, nor just about breaking down taboos. Those are methods to the end goal, of just being, the middle way. Whole.

Part 4: The Skeptical Buddha

"If you see an intelligent man who tells you where true treasures are to be found, who shows what is to be avoided, and points out your faults, follow that wise man; it will be better, not worse, for those who follow him."

"One who conquers himself is greater than another who conquers a thousand times a thousand men on the battlefield. Be victorious over yourself and not over others. When you attain victory over yourself, not even the gods can turn it into defeat."

– Gautama Buddha (Dhammapada)

Mindful Meditation

One of the quintessential science-based books on the subject of mindfulness is published out of the University of Massachusetts called Mindfulness by Mark Williams and Danny Penman. This book had a dramatic impact on my life and mental wellbeing. Their studies involved taking various forms of traditional meditation and changing it up and stripping it down to find out what parts of the Buddhists tradition are beneficial and what parts are just superstitions carrying on as extra baggage. Previous studies using functional magnetic resonance imaging (fMRI) have correlated a lighting up of the left prefrontal cortex corresponding with a person's happiness and the right prefrontal cortex linked to more sadness or depression. fMRI shows that there is a very high success rate after using the 8-week mindful meditation technique, of switching the primary use from the right to the left. On top of all the other benefits, it has also been shown to cause an antibody boost as empathy increases as well as lowered cortisol, which are very good for the immune system.

Unlike animals that can stop thinking about stress when it's not present, humans have imagination and can cause themselves panic even when no danger is present just from speculation alone. Your thoughts affect sensations. You think about something you are worried about, and you tense up. This physical feedback affects your feelings and impulses, your fight or flight response

must learn to stop chasing your tail.

This low happiness cycle is just natural but can cause self-abuse and discontentment. If your first reaction is anger, it can create blind rage, blocking outside-the-box creativity and thinking. All other options will close off and you will beat your head against a brick wall trying one way over and over again to fix something, making yourself even more frustrated. You must train a natural alarm to go off to the realization that other alternatives may be available when you get stuck. Being tired and hungry will cause this problem as well. Most people don't stop and consider that "maybe I'm just hungry" when they feel unwell. Most people will focus on feeling awful in the moment and either blame themselves or the situation.

They tell an old story in Mindfulness of a child with a stubborn mule. Nothing he can do will make the mule go. His grandfather comes out and tells him to stop. Then the grandfather puts his face next to the mule and looks down the road to show it where he wants it to go. A minute later when the mule is calmed, he starts walking, much to the boy's delight. I like to compare the lizard brain to an animal and our conscious mind as the one who is trying to tame it. It will do things it's evolved to do, not necessarily what we want it to do. My youtube series "Training Your Inner Beast" goes further into detail on this, using animal training techniques we can use on our own mind.

and your emotions, making you less happy. Quite often this goes back to affecting your thoughts and you wonder why you aren't happier and your brain tries to logically figure out how or why it's unhappy using up brain power. Then it compares its happiness level to better times, making the cycle cause even more unhappiness. Essentially, you

Much of our life is like that. Instead of learning the mechanism of our mind and how to get our inner beast to do what we want, we beat it up. We compare ourselves to others which makes us despise ourselves even more.

If we don't ignore or rationalize the difference between our ideal and our real self, we often attack ourselves because we compare the two and they are never the same. We beat ourselves up making it worse, ensuring we will never get where we want to be. My therapist told me at one point that I thought too black and white, so I was never content. Not only about myself but about reality and that crippled me because I was so overwhelmed and exhausted from empathy that I was essentially helpless and useless at making actual change. She told me that what I needed to do was to take my ideal and move my expectations midway toward reality to a new center. After achieving that, then I might not be as overwhelmed, and it was piecemeal enough to begin change. A journey of a thousand miles begins with just one step – Lao Tzu. If you can't take that first step you are just as useless to the cause as an apathetic person.

You must look at things as they are, not as how you think they should be. One of the key components of Mindful meditation is accepting reality, even if it's painful. Quite often your brain tries to fight or ignore pain that you have. It seems counterintuitive but trying to fight or ignore the pain often uses more brain energy, preventing your brain from processing and adjusting to the pain. Pain is a strange creature and your perception of it seriously is affected by your mood

A soldier shot but not fatally with the ticket to go home after serving his country will feel a lot less pain than a person with liver cancer who may or may not survive. How the pain was caused, how much of which emotion is linked to it, and other factors will affect how the pain is perceived (Beecher, 1956). Mentally resisting the pain can often cause the pain to hurt worse than just accepting and acknowledging the pain thereby freeing up brain space. However, our superstitious-wired minds often assume that if we resist it and try to ignore it and believe it doesn't hurt, we can magically make it go away. The Buddha referred to this as two darts, the dart of the initial injury and then the second dart is caused by ourselves trying to fight or ignore the first one.

Acceptance in the moment instead of using judgment is not fatalistic, though many people may be worried that is how it works so they often never think to do it. Focusing on the future and how things should be is important, but focusing on how things aren't, too much, can wear your brain out and lead to burnout.

Another important issue is the effects of memory and ties to negative and positive emotions. Objects and habits can all tie to memories, either positive or negative. As it turns out, memories can influence accessing other memories. Negative thinking makes it harder to access good memories and dreams of the future, which makes being happy or positive thinking even harder to achieve. Mindfulness discusses methods for breaking routines and doing things differently to be able to better access new memories and make it more difficult to access negative memories.

They have exercises to make you aware of what they call your Autopilot, or your limbic inner beast, or your reactive mind. You often do basic things running purely on automatic without ever thinking about it with your reflective mind. One exercise is the raisin or chocolate meditation. The raisin requires you to sit and slowly eat a raisin or other small foods, paying close attention to each step and what sensations you are feeling and what thoughts and emotions are occurring in your mind. Treat it as if you were a baby with no linked memories or perceived ideas about it. Just play with the sensations, not as life has programmed you to think about them by giving them words or descriptors but enjoy the sensation without thinking about any ties to anything else as if you have no other memories to compare it to.

These exercises teach your inner beast to be calm and focused. The problem is not that you are relying on your inner

beast to do things, the problem is that the inner beast will often volunteer for jobs it is not suited for at all, and if you are running on automatic you will eagerly let it try, and often fail.

"Habit releasers," are tricks to go about changing normal daily patterns that will change your memory connections. This will give you a different perspective, thereby giving you the ability to create new memories. An example is a 15-minute walk, perhaps in an area you've never walked, without rush and paying attention to the sensations you are receiving. Another is just switching chairs at the dinner table that you usually sit in. Something as small as that can change the memory process of the experience

Most people don't know how to adjust their mood depending on the situation, so when they are in a good mood, which can be rare, many don't use it to look at painful issues that need fixing while they have the nurtured feelings and energy to tackle them. Many people use alcohol this way as well, causing a lot of problems. Fixing it would cause a lot more long-term happiness, but right now they want to be happy. They don't want to spend the time and energy focusing on negative experiences or thoughts. In a sense, they go numb or "brainless" to the negative aspects of their lives. Also, since they can't adjust their mood, when they finally pull themselves out of a bad situation, their brains can't adjust to the lack of stress, so they make more drama and sabotage themselves and their potential happiness in the process. If someone has been beating their inner beast too long, they won't feel like they deserve good things happening to them.

On the flip side, I have known people who think they can just work through their mental health issues like a workaholic and end up burning themselves out and crippling themselves, never giving their brain a break to enjoy anything. This ends up just making the problem and the depression even worse and they are working so hard and just getting worse and worse. This leads to more self abuse and self-hatred for not living up to one's supposed standards and end up like the Buddha feeling guilty over having just a grain of rice, or a moment of pleasure, and will end up drowning themselves from emotional malnutrition. A healthy middle ground is needed, sadly if they knew how to do that they might not have the problems to begin with.

Psychologists have discovered that much of this trapped past thinking comes down to the memory response that is common in most people when tired. These people, when depressed or suffering after a traumatic event, when asked to recall specific memories that make them feel emotions, end up stopping after the first stage of memory retrieval, lumping many similar concepts with memories. The brain stops short of being able to state anything specific. When a depressed person with this memory

problem is asked to name a specific time and event that made them happy, they can't. They will just say something like, "My friends and I used to go out on weekends." They can't remember specific times associated with positive or negative memories, they just all run together. Overgeneralized memory is more prevalent with less psychologically resilient people who, instead of remembering things in more detail, will remember the past items rather vaguely as just "all bad." From then on, any time they think about that part of their past it leads to negative thinking no matter how prevalent those past experiences.

Your inner beast is great at spreading rumors and propaganda, making you feel like you can't do anything or the world or your life is worse than it is. Generalized memory prevents you from letting go of the past, locking you into it and making sure you can't live your life in the now.

If you are one who is too focused on past mistakes, you can never move on. Mistakes are only bad when nothing is learned, most of the greatest people learned everything that was important to their success from a lot of failure. Sadly, we've been given the illusion by well-choreographed media that if we fail a first time or many times there is something wrong with us.

The only purpose of fear is self-preservation, the only purpose of anger is action, the only purpose of guilt is change, the only purpose of desire should be motivation. If you have done these, and not having these emotions wont do anything to change what you are currently doing then letting go of these past emotions is essential to moving forward in life.

When you are stressed out, studies show that you are more likely to believe inaccurate lies you tell yourself, either good or bad. Which is why you get angry at others because you feel superior or feel like crap because you think you are inferior. It also makes you more likely to be blindsided by your own biases and believe without thinking. This will lock you in a cycle of delusion that is very damaging.

One misconception made by many people is that meditation is about clearing the mind. This causes them to get frustrated and fretful when they can't clear their mind because they are stressing out so much that they aren't completing this unspecified task. A cleared mind is a product of meditation, much like a strong body is a product of weightlifting. Your brain is changing and rewriting pathways as you meditate and increasing brain mass and neural connections. The process may not be fun at first, just like with weightlifting, but as you progress, you will begin to enjoy it more and more as you begin to see results.

The psychologists in Mindfulness have found that the best meditators are ones who have a willingness to experiment with their minds as it is important practice in non-judgement. You will find your thoughts and emotions fluctuate or as they

call it "emotional weather." Many people beat themselves up over this, as they forget that peace and calm is an end achievement like gaining muscle and not the process like working out. The best meditators are ones who have the skill of being ok with starting over when their minds drift. Meditation failure is just practice, and you need to learn to accept that it will happen.

Unfortunately, the more you need meditation, the less likely you are to remember to do it. So often you need to plan mini meditations. Many experience dread at the thought of having to stop and take time out of their busy rushed schedule for meditation, but it can prevent error and worse problems. A little maintenance and mindfulness here and there can make your life a whole lot happier.

One hot summer day, the Buddha was walking through the forest. He began to feel very thirsty. He asked Ananda, "Remember that small stream three or four miles back?

Please take my begging bowl and bring back some water for me. I am thirsty and tired."

Ananda went back but a bullock cart had just passed through the stream and churned the water up, making it extremely muddy. Dead leaves that had settled on the bed had been stirred up and floated on the surface. No one could drink that water.

He returned to his master empty handed.

"I am sorry, Master, but you will have to wait. That water is undrinkable. I have heard there is a stream two miles up the road, let's just move forward and get some then."

But the Buddha was insistent, "Go back and bring water from that stream."

Bewildered, he headed back out again. If his master said so, Ananda felt that there must be some reason. As he was leaving, the Buddha said, "And don't come back if the water is still dirty. If it is, simply sit on the bank silently. Don't do anything. Don't get into the stream. Sit and watch silently. Soon, the water will become clear, and you can fill the bowl and come back."

Ananda got to the stream and realized his master was right. It was getting clearer, but not clear enough to drink so he sat on the side and watched. It suddenly struck him why his master was so insistent. This was a lesson for him. The water over time became crystal clear.

He came back to his master, excited, and thanked him.

"Why are you thanking me? You brought me water; I should be thanking you." "I understand. I was angry at the moment, although I hid it from you. I thought you were just being stubborn and not listening to me when you sent me back because it was absurd. But I understand the message now and it's just what I needed. I sat on the bank and realized it is the same with my mind. If I jump into the stream, I will make it dirty again. If I jump into my mind, more noise and mess is created, making more problems surface. Sitting on the side and observing has taught me a new technique.

"Now I will sit by the side of my mind, watching the swirling mess and chaos, old hurts, wounds and regrets, memories and desires. Unconcerned, I will sit on the banks of my mind and observe, waiting for the moment when all is clear."

Buddhism for Skeptics

The interesting thing about Buddhism is that much of the barebones philosophy has been proven to be scientific. Or at least the parts that can be studied and it has been embraced by the psychological community. That is one of the enduring legacies of such a rich and robust study. The group prayer at mass, the chants of the Gregorian and the Imam at the mosque, confessions, which acted as psychology sessions, all of these had positive benefits that made us feel a part of something bigger than ourselves. This is something that we as individuals have been missing since we grew as a species out of our hunter/gatherer lifestyle and the world and population exploded beyond

our comprehension. There are pieces of Buddhism that are incredibly helpful and profound, especially in each of the schools. However, each of them was trapped by dogma and biases that they didn't know they had and ignorance they couldn't possibly know until science became more and more perfected. There is a very real way to strip out the dregs of ignorance using science and skepticism and find and embrace the parts that we can prove and can help us in our daily lives.

Unlike Gautama Siddartha, we have that power which he never could have. And we can move forward to perfect his ideas, training ourselves to be skeptical but, as with enlightenment, possibly never reaching it, because it is a journey not an ending, and the second we think we've ended our journey, pride will muck it all up. Blasphemy with an equal mix of humility leads to enlightenment, and the same is true with skepticism. Sadly many self-declared skeptics often think the blasphemy alone makes them skeptical, but are oblivious to the importance of humility or you won't question your own biases.

What Many Get Wrong about Buddhism

Upon requestioning Buddhism I began to develop several problems I found with it. It turns out many of those "flaws" were common misunderstandings, especially as The Guru presented a sadly over simplified version of Buddhism as did many western books based off of earlier texts that were not as well nuanced. It turns out, these are common criticisms of Buddhism by many outsiders, when they aren't actually part of the doctrine at all, although some sects may practice them.

Buddhism and Fatalism

Many believe that Buddhism often treats the problems of reality as inevitable to the point that they are kind of fatalistic about suffering in the world and not attempting to change the system. It is true that prior to science, there wasn't a lot you could do to change the human experience externally, however that was true about most religions. In this day and age we have the tools to fix the problems even if it requires desiring change to motivate effort. This "fatalistic" Buddhism is viewed by many as nihilistic, because everything is morally relative. And if that is the way you wish to live, checking out from reality and accepting the suffering

around you as just normal, that is your call. However, this is completely counter to any form of modern humanism where each generation can live better and better lives, each tackling a new set of issues, but passing these benefits on to the next generation.

That said, most of the teachings of the Buddha discuss changing yourself and how you perceive the world just as modern scientific psychology does. This is a confusion of Buddhism especially among its critics and even some of its practitioners. .

Enlightenment is supposedly a state where you have no desires at all, and nothing can affect you in this mortal plane because it does not matter. You are waiting for your mortal body to release you, but you also do not desire it. Nothing rocks you, makes you angry or sad. You are calm and at peace with the world, and see everything as connected and how the flow of the universe works. Everything in the world is as it should be at this point in time.

Aiming toward this can be good with countering stress, and over reaction to inconvenience, however when taken dogmatically can be kind of appalling. Many monks isolated themselves from the common people to reach this as a special class instead of working to advance humanity. They locked themselves away from injustice and brutalities, ignoring suffering, privileged in their revered status as holy men. The Tibetan monks ruled over their peasants in rather brutal ways to live in luxury while their people struggled. Dali Lama Tenzin may have continued the practice had China not forced him out and began implementing cultural genocide being also isolated and privileged from the normal world as this was "just the way things were." This experience changed his entire view on reality, opening his mind up and dealing directly with his people as opposed to living as a god-king.

Mind you, as stated before, without science at the time, there was no true good way to advance and reduce the needless suffering of humanity., Bad kings were natural, empires fell, famine was natural, Death and destruction is everywhere and common, Children died at a rate of 3 out of 5. Human life is cheap. Suffering is normal. Reality is suffering.

With Science, we've improved the human condition. People don't die as much, famine and starvation is declining. Natural disasters continue to kill less people thanks to early warning systems (though they are increasing due to the marriage of science and politics creating global climate change). The amount of people killed in war continues to decline in spite of the media blasting us with so many conflicts to choose from. Per person, the violence rate is dropping yearly across the globe. But we still have a lot of work to do if we want to reach a place of any form of justice and peace. We must work to reorganize power structures and financial

structures and continue to increase scientific inquiry. When life is truly hopeless, "enlightenment" state is a wonderful way to live.

Until 100 years ago, most suffering just was, but we now have the means to eliminate much of the needless suffering and going to a permanently isolationist "enlightenment" state is just selfish. The only way for evil to triumph is for good people to do nothing. Mahayana and Vajrayana Buddhism addressed this more clearly and were concerned with it, believing that empathy was one of the most powerful forces in the world, but the double ended dagger was used to symbolize empathy as when you hurt someone else you also hurt yourself.

There is even the question of the psychological impacts of too much meditation and isolation that in some studies show could potentially lead to narcissism. Mind you, this problem is similar to our current question of "is too much exercise like running a marathon actually unhealthy?" (Horgan, 2011). Most of us will never get the amount of exercise or meditation we need for this to ever become an issue.

There are also cases where people took this to an extreme and self-mummified as the ultimate act of asceticism and denial of desires (Baklitskaya, 2015) . It was believed if this occurred he would become a Buddha. This led them to eat certain types of wood chips and salt until their body ultimately became a mummy. Their body was enshrined and the body was believed to be still alive and the now Buddha was enlightened that the world had stopped for him but still lived among them. This kind of ideal of enlightenment taken to a suicidal level is based on dogma, not on anything the Buddha actually said. But, just like in the desire for immortality, the desire to be most anything, can lead to destruction.

Rationalizing of violence

While most people view Buddhism as a clear religion of peace, once it made its way into political power, they figured out some nice work arounds so they could still be Buddhist and be violent. Sometimes they would say that you can commit violence but ensure your intentions are pure and that is what matters most. Buddhist nationalism in the modern era in Thailand and Sri Lanka have led to some violent wars. While a fear of the Rohingya Muslims in Myanmar led to a massacre that made the already marginalized Muslims flee en masse to live stateless lives in refugee camps.

Facebook, at the time of these massacres, had a system to create free Wi-Fi. However, it was limited to a handful of websites that included Facebook. This ended up being the only source of information on the Rohingya Muslims. With this chokehold of information, the military and certain Buddhist monks stoked fear and hatred of the marginalized Muslims. They were given the

tools of information without being given the tools to distinguish good information from the bad.

Buddhism also integrates with other folk religions, and just fills in the gaps of what their folk religion didn't provide like with Bon in Tibet, Religious Taoism in China and Shinto in Japan, and one religion may override and rationalize violence over the other. While it might be considered one of the most peaceful religions, just like any religion, it can be twisted to rationalize war and terrible violence.

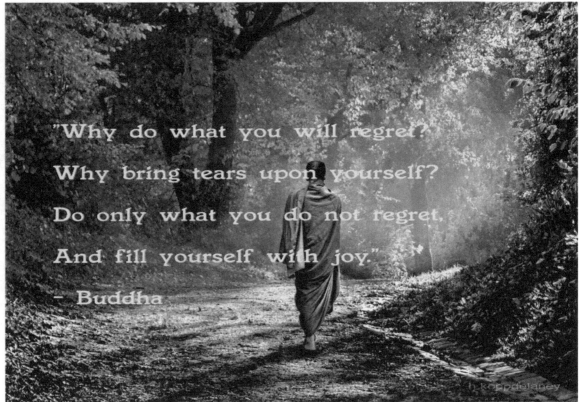

"Why do what you will regret?
Why bring tears upon yourself?
Do only what you do not regret,
And fill yourself with joy."
- Buddha

What Buddhism got wrong

Buddhism as a religion should not be judged on the same merits as Buddhism as a philosophy. Buddhism, the philosophy, also should not be judged by modern current knowledge. A religion is meant to require faith many times in the face of evidence against it. A philosophy, especially an applied philosophy, is supposed to make life better for the practitioner. So, was philosophical Buddhism right about making one's life better through its practice?

No science at the time

Buddhism was a philosophy of the times. It was the best they could do in those days, and it did quite well for thousands of years. They even touched on the idea of biases but didn't know the details to which our

biases exist or the cause. They understood that our brain chemicals act like drugs at times that cloud our vision and our decision making. They also had no systematic method to be skeptical and to discover the truth of the world and discard bad ideas that we now have in science. Scientists are now finding things out about Buddhism such as meditation lowering blood pressure, changing your brain, reducing pain and other positive benefits. For a philosophy with no modern science it is actually quite scientific, which is impressive. However, bad ideas still got into the mix that plagued it.

Reincarnation

Most schools of Buddhism still believe in some form of rebirth or reincarnation. This was the core need for breaking the cycle of Samsara. In the process they began adding other ideas onto it, and some were able to break away from that idea entirely. This is similar to how algebra was invented because Islamic law for splitting inheritance was a complete nightmare, so they ended up taking Greek and Indian mathematics and fusing them, creating a new form of math that went on to have way more uses. Most cultures discarded the ties to the original problem from the religion it was first meant to solve.

In modern Skeptical Buddhism, without solid evidence for reincarnation or an afterlife, anyone can now discard these ideas if they so choose. They can still function and move on to perform other tasks for their life if they find it to be useful. The idea of reincarnation to help people gain empathy for the problems of the world and to fix it for the next one no longer are coupled with that idea of reincarnation and the afterlife. It can be accomplished in this life.

It can still be a death philosophy

Pretty much all religions and philosophies are created to help you deal with death. As the age we live grows longer and longer and science produces life extension and other methods of fighting or possibly even eliminating aging, many of the Buddhist ideas may lose their importance. That is also true for most religions except in times of duress, accidents, or untreatable diseases.

Neil deGrasse Tyson has repeated

like so many have before him, the idea being this: if there was a pill you could take to extend life indefinitely, he would not take it. He feels his sense of wonder would be diminished and his urgency that drives him to do great things would be depleted.

I personally do not understand this concept. Death is not a driver for me, it is a depressor and creates nihilism and lethargy for me. Or it drives me to focus on dealing with the fear of death via meditation and acceptance which makes me neutral in terms of drive. I haven't got to do so many things I wanted to do in life, mostly due to limited options and limited finances as well as a broad range of interests. Neil had a bullseye focus on what he loves but it is impossible for me to love just one field enough to do what he did. Also, I don't believe that constant work is either good or natural, unless it's something we are 100% passionate about, and even then, slowing down can create richer results in the long run or we can get burnt out.

For the first time ever, death may be a choice in our lifetime, which scares a lot of people when you talk to them about it. All our ideas, religions and philosophies focus on death and dealing with death. Most of them were founded back when our life expectancy was half of what it is today, and we didn't have a lot of time to think. They are sadly outdated as I know so many teens that focus on death and have no sense of wonder because all their philosophies are based around death, they don't know how to enjoy life, especially in the age of climate change and the constant fluctuations in the economy. I myself recommend a life philosophy and a death philosophy. The danger is when you are hooked on one and the other sneaks up on you and causes you terrible fear because you don't have a philosophy to deal with it.

Back when life was short and death was certain and often, focusing on death was very important. When I reach death, I will focus back on the philosophies of death to gain solace.
What we need are philosophies of life now to drive us to become better people and make the world into a place where one would enjoy living forever. I believed that death philosophy most of my life leading me to a lot of depression. I now have a level of wonder and excitement about my life, my opportunities and what will be discovered. The more I know, the more I want to know, as new knowledge creates new questions.

I am not driven by my sense of death as that would just lead me to stress out, killing me much sooner, reducing what I could be capable of doing with more wisdom and better understanding. I am driven to ensure that I am worthy of a longer life, that I deserve the gift given me. The philosophy of life requires creating and maintaining wonder, that is what will keep you motivated

and going, with a more flexible mind. (Zabelina, 2010)

Unless we all work to improve the system and take on some of the stress and desire of the world, others won't have the luxury to reduce their stress and desires. The cycle of enlightenment and Mindful Meditation seem to be the only truly selfless form of Buddhism for a skeptic. Of course some may say that it's not real Buddhism, but considering there is a branch that believes that the way to Nirvana is through Christian-like faith in the Buddha, and He wrote down nothing and had 32 disciples that all started schools with different ideas, I'm going to say that that would be a No True Scotsman fallacy.

Relaxation, emptiness and peace are valuable but also luxuries. Taking on the stresses of the world for a time is the only way to truly have what the Buddhists consider the most powerful force in the universe. Empathy.

That said, of all the religions and applied philosophies, Buddhism is probably one of the most flexible of all of them. There is a reason why so many great thinkers have believed that Buddhism will in the end win out, as it is at its very core a philosophy of rationality, and assumes nothing except for what can be discovered. Discomforts, disappointments, desires and sufferings will still exist just for much longer stretches of time without death. Also with the option of

not dying people could be driven to be even more fearful of dying as they could have thousands of years ahead of them instead of decades. Non-attachment to the desire for life will be an essential part of possible immortality or mental health and sanity will not exist and the extended life will just be extended suffering, not extended joy and opportunity.

Buddhism will end up marrying itself with new philosophies for how to deal with immortality just as it did for Shinto, Bon, and Taoism, filling in the gaps or acting as a starting point for a new form of Immortalist philosophy to spring forth. We haven't had that luxury yet, however the Chinese Taoists contemplated the idea a lot as they believed immortality was attainable just like Western alchemists. And that will be another philosophy that will blend with Buddhism, and Humanism to birth Immortalism when we have reached that point to have that luxury.

My own experiences with Buddhism

I lived out in the country where I was homeschooled. We had one car most of the time that my dad used. I had a lot of free time growing up and little socializing. Because of a combo of Asperger's and evangelical religion and a lot of reflective time, I was able to be very mindful to the point of depression because I could see all the bad in the world and didn't have a clue how to train my reflexive mind to do anything.
I had a high appreciation for the world and a great wonder about it. My brother always wondered how I could talk about, focus on, and see all the horribleness in the world and not go out and kill myself because talking to me usually ended up depressing him. Unlike most people who were great at the doing but

not great at the being, I was the exact opposite. I ignored my beast and never utilized it, as the beast made me sin. Most people run via their beast and rarely let their reflective minds do work other than possibly to beat their inner beast.

I wore my reflective mind out trying to be aware of everything and never let my inner beast do what it was there for. As it never got practice, it made doing anything more difficult than it should've been and I wondered why my life was so much harder than anyone around me. Once I learned self-hypnosis and relaxation I got in touch with my inner beast, and I was able to do twice as much if not more because I didn't have to be mindful constantly.

Because of this weird combination I took to Buddhism and what I believe to be enlightenment very easily. However, the empathy I felt and increased from it made me feel guilty for having this happiness that others couldn't have. When the Buddha first discovered enlightenment, he basically became dirt poor and had his followers do the same. They travelled around and stayed at people's houses and begged for food and in exchange taught people spiritual teaching. In an age of high illiteracy, this was not a bad deal for the average laborer.

However, the contentment experienced by enlightenment was caused by a position of privilege. Most of these laborers didn't have the time or energy to reach enlightenment, however without them the monks couldn't live that lifestyle. It was probably the best system for the time but sadly unfair now and we live in a system these days where we all have access to information and none of us can fairly live off the rest of the world and avoid stress.

As we progress we must think of life itself as a living reincarnation. Each time you discover or rediscover enlightenment you are dying and being reborn, much like a time lord regeneration from Doctor Who. At 25 I had ambitious plans to help the world and I knew the only way to do so would be to get a degree at that time to increase my income from what I was making. It required me to leave my contentment behind and step out and deal with stress. I was happy, I could have lived the rest of my life contented, had the economy continued on its path. But I saw the horrors of the world around me and knew I couldn't stand by and be the only one loving life. It feels a lot like being in heaven while knowing others are in hell.

Thanks to the economy, those plans were ruined and, in the process, I discovered that I probably don't have the skills needed for that plan. Now my main goal is to get out of student loan debt and become financially stable again like I was before I decided to take on my plans. Now I am working to return to my state of contentment so I can regroup my efforts and re-energize my sense of wonder and empathy. My reserves of these are a lot lower than they used to be, especially with the current political and economic climate.

After you have accomplished your goal or failed and learned experience, then return to awakened contentment to regroup. You now have the mental clarity to come up with a much better plan and analyze all options than you would have stressed out about until you can sit on the side of your mind and reality, not interacting, until your thoughts settle and you can see a clear path forward to try with the most chances of causing real change.

Without trying new things you are often ignorant just how your ideal and real selves differ because that part of you has never been challenged. Without pushing yourself and experimenting with your reactive self you will never know if all the effort you put in with your reflective self actually worked and you will live in more delusion that you are closer to your ideal self than you actually are.

Buddhism, at its core, will survive these new changes as it always has been like water on the rocks of time because as I quoted at the beginning.

"If scientific analysis were conclusively to demonstrate certain claims in Buddhism to be false, then we must accept the findings of science and abandon those claims." - The 14th Dali Lama

The Tao of Science

An Introduction to Taoism

"Free from desire, you realize the mystery. Caught in desire, you see only the manifestations."

This verse from the Tao Te Ching's first section points to the very basic needs of a scientist to understand reality and find the truth. If you desire an outcome or want to discover something quickly, you will almost always find the wrong conclusion. Science is viewed by the outsider as a bunch of discoveries that make our lives better. Inside of science there are a lot of boring failures and only a small percentage of them are useful, but those failures are worth all the effort. As my partner Archyfantasies put it, "Science is simultaneously the most interesting and most boring thing ever."

Science is tedious. Collection of data is tedious. Repeating experiments is tedious and often there are people who go through their entire career only discovering what can't be done, or only making modest advances in a field.

The desire for flash and fame has plagued science for decades, all the way back to the alchemists of old. Today, case studies and journals require someone being impressed, either for charities, companies with financial stakes, wealthy donors, or even the Government.

Today, case studies and journals require someone being impressed, either for charities, companies with financial stakes, wealthy donors, or even the Government. They need to be wowed with results, even though science funding should equally fund the most boring of studies as much as the ones with immediate, real-world results.

Boring research will generate data that could be critical in helping a scientist in the future have some massive breakthrough. You will see on the news, politicians bashing funding going to the mating habits of a particular species of snail as trivial and a waste of taxpayer money, however if that snail turns out to be the perfect animal model for a specific disease or drug pathway in the future or to produce a certain chemical, that research that seemed useless at the time will benefit humanity to no end.

An intimate friend of 19th century physicist Michael Faraday once described how, when Faraday was endeavoring to explain to Prime Minister William Gladstone and several others an important new discovery in science involving electricity, Gladstone's only commentary was 'but, after all, what use is it?'

'Why, sir,' replied Faraday. 'There is every probability that you will soon be able to tax it!' This desire for fame has led scientists to release really bad papers, such as the Japanese scientist Haruko Obokata who faked data about a stem cell transformation through a mild acid bath technique that would have changed medicine entirely. If it hadn't been both flashy and easy, it's quite possible that the study would have never been reproduced and proven to be wrong. The need to publish or perish to receive funding has driven scientists to avoid replicating other people's experiments to double check their work and to only work on new research. This has created a reproducibility crisis and up to 50% of papers in some fields of science were unable to be reproduced. While these flawed papers are not enough to overturn central dogma and theories of the field, they can waste time and money on future studies that would have never been conducted if they hadn't used the prior research to assume the new research was a plausible idea.

The strong desire of the scientist for success can also blind them with bias to see patterns or results that don't actually exist which is why the peer review process is essential. It is why pseudo-scientists claim oppression by the scientific community, as more eyes with no emotional or financial horse in the race are needed to see the research impartially to decide if an idea or study has merit. All the while, pseudo-scientists are the most biased you can get where they begin with a premise and cherry pick the data to find the data that helps them, while ignoring all of the data that doesn't. You see only the result and never the cause.

Part 1: What is Taoism?

Taoism and its meaning get murky very quickly, especially to a modern Western mind where, like Buddhism, it can mean both a religion and a philosophy. The religion of Taoism is akin to Japanese Shinto, an ancestor worshipping religion, with gods, and animistic spirits and the abilities to understand and gain supernatural powers.

Taoism the philosophy is believed to have become a rejection of legalism while Lao Tzu was alleged to be alive and the philosophy evolved into a backlash against Confucianism after Lao Tzu died. It was anti-modernist, anti-legalist, pro-nature, and pro-self determination to an extent. As I said in the first half of the book, as a political philosophy it was like their version of the American libertarian party and the green party combined.

The Tao just means "the way" but the term was meant to encompass everything about the entire universe and reality. It was so massive and complex, similar to the Hindu concept of Brahma, it could never be put into words, though one could follow a path to better understand it if you could train your mind to think about it on its rules and terms, not on your own rules usually put upon you via society. Golden Age syndrome of hating on modernity was at the cornerstone of early philosophical Taoism.

The Tao is the way, the way is much more important than the end goal. Focusing on the end goal is viewed as silly and laughable because the way is most often so different from what you expected that you may be so hung up on the goal, which may not be achievable that you miss other paths of opportunity that you could be taking instead. The way of the universe, acting less as a force that leaves an impact and more like water. Change, especially big change, comes much slower and much more organic through unexpected ways than we realize. Setting out to discover something is difficult. You can set up a starting hypothesis and a methodology you will use, but then once you get the data, if you only think about it as how you first hypothesized as yes or no you can completely miss nuance or possibly other discoveries that were side effects of just trying to do something that hadn't been done before.

That is true in life as well. Life rarely goes the way you would like. By being flexible and observant as to how the situation is flowing, you can better act, nudging the flow of events as opposed to forcefully changing them. Action through non-action, or the least action, making the least impact possible is the best method for living according to the Tao. Judo is about reading the flow and using the opponent's move against them through physics. Taoism is about waiting, watching and discovering the least invasive and energy consuming method of causing the biggest change.

Invention was rarely something people set out to do, or if they did, they more often than not failed. While we hear about the first person to discover something, it was actually many people working on the problem and sharing ideas, slowly, gradually and organically evolving. There were many people looking at the idea

for the most part, but we only hear about the one who figured out the puzzle first, never the person who came in second place. Not unless there was a dispute for personal or political reasons. Discovery and progress are so much more organic and require more people ignored by history than the narrative will let you know.

If the end goal is more important than the way, and the end is so much more emotional to you than the way it was discovered, you can easily be susceptible to bias and get the wrong answer because you started out with a goal first and decided that it was true instead of going where the data led. Stalin believed that with sheer force of will the Soviet Union could solve any scientific problem. Because of this he believed in a dogmatic pseudo-scientist Trofim Lysenko and believed a post scarcity age of Communism by full automation was just around the corner with so much plentiful food that they would have to overeat just to keep up with the supply of food. That robots for all and the elimination of scarcity would occur in 20-50 years, so they should all sacrifice now and give in to the grueling labor and draconian laws he set down to achieve this glorious future.

Because of this belief, millions of Ukrainians died, requiring signs telling them that cannibalism is wrong, and millions more were worked to death in gulags. Stalin spread this ideology to Mao which led to the

140

great leap forward killing millions as well. Probably the most extreme example of the failings that can happen from trying to use brute force against nature. It wasn't until Stalin died that they realized his cult-like ideas were ludicrous and the Soviet Union turned to much more practical and realistic solutions to scientific problems. Once they began looking at what the rest of the world was doing and decided to take a much more organic route the people of the Soviet Union began to enjoy some prosperity and security, as well as being the first nation to go to space.

The industrial revolution caused a great deal of positive change, but it moved so fast with profit as the end goal that many side effects were incurred. Many workers lost their lives, either through neglect, overwork, pollution or strike breaking. This is not following the Tao either.

The Tao finds the least invasive or impactful way to create the most change but to leave the smallest footprint.

Everyone has a path. Everyone's journey is different. If you have an end goal, even a small one, the path is probably much different than you imagined and like Murphy's law states, if anything can go wrong it will. The way does not make value judgments. Most people will look at a pot as just the clay that was used to make it, a Taoist will also look at the space that makes up the interior of the vessel as equally important.

In engineering, materials and their properties are neither good nor bad, but good or bad depending on what the need is. One material may be utterly awful for one job, but perfect for another. For every benefit in a material there is always a drawback. The harder a substance, the more brittle it is, the more flexible the weaker it is to distortion. The whole can become greater than the sum of the parts. A material with carbon fibers in it, just due to their reinforcement can add strength and reduce brittleness to a material. There is no good or bad, but about more or less beneficial for a situation which is often much more complex than a black and white of good and bad.

Most religions have an end goal, salvation or some reward you are trying to attain. For Taoism the way is the reward. Spontaneity and genuineness, not structured or socially acceptable. Any untruth can blind you to an opportunity or how the world actually works. Like a leaf on the wind, you go with the flow and spot opportunities as you go without focusing on the end goal. This is why it's viewed more as a philosophy than a religion, even though the philosophy is bound to the religion so much that the Chinese folk religion shares its name.

We shall start with the religion of Taoism which predates the philosophy of Taoism. It's hard to understand how they are intertwined and when the philosophy came from otherwise.

The Evolution of Taoism

Taoism as a religion is generally the cultural religion of China. It is different through the ages and through each part of the nation, but without understanding the most basic history of the religion as a foundation, understanding the philosophy's origins will be difficult to grasp.

The Shang Dynasty was the first dynasty in China for whose existence we have real evidence. The king was the spiritual leader and performed the ceremonies and sacrifices needed for the nation to thrive under the gods. They had a pantheon similar to all pagan religions at the time, and being an old bronze age civilization, the past was almost always better than the present.

The previous Xia dynasty, which is probably more based in myth than reality, mimicked the Greek heroic age in writing where the kings were always wise and all kings since have fallen into selfishness and foolishness. From Yu the Great who gained

Kingship from the merit of his ability to tame the Yellow river through locks and levees and irrigation, to the wondrous Yellow Emperor who is considered the bastion of nobility and pretty much the inventor of every modern convenience of that age.

The main purpose of a philosopher was an attempt to figure out what they had lost with modernity to lose that philosopher kingship and Arthurian nobility who legend told of. An even higher bar were the god kings who came before them of the three pure ones including the venerable Jade Emperor.

The Shang worshipped their ancestors, sought signs and advice from diviners just like most other people during that time period. Turtle shells were used for divinations based on how they cracked which archaeologists have found with the first Chinese writing on it from as early as 1200 BCE.

When the Shang dynasty ended, the Zhou dynasty rose with King Wu around 1046 BCE. Kings were considered divine and given the blessing of heaven, so when King Wu seized the throne, he had to rationalize it. With help from astrologers and divination experts he invented the political philosophy of the Mandate of Heaven that gods only gave the right to rule to kings who pleased them and were good kings for the people. When omens and signs came about, like ones that had happened before his rise to power, that meant that Heaven was displeased with the current administration and the dynasty could be overthrown.

Upon the inevitable slow breakdown of the Zhou empire, during the "Spring and Autumn period" where power slowly became more and more decentralized, the former knights, or Ru – similar to late era Samurai – lost their backing and legitimacy. They now had to use their education and knowledge to either find lords to become advisors to, or start their own schools of thought to teach others and debate with each other. This was done in hopes of gaining merit to win the potential to be sponsored by a king or lord, with the hope of discovering the missing piece that separated the Xia noble kings from the modern brutal and

corrupt kings.

From this change we got the Hundred Schools of Thought. This was the time when the most expansion of Thought happened in China from around 770 BCE to 221 at the end of the warring states period. Ideas were tested, debated and argued between many different philosophers similar to what was occuring in Greece and India at the time. Gathering in cities, especially ones with systems of writing, allowed for people, for the first time, to exchange and debate new ideas about life, the universe, and everything. Organizing thought and logic was an essential part of getting to the truth. Of course, just like in Greece, pagan

traditions and divinations continued. So that much of the more popular schools were not asking "where did things come from," and questions about the gods, but about how to get back to the wonderful societies of the Xia and how to organize a society and pick a king who was going to be like Yu the Great or the Yellow emperor. They were seeking a utopia that never was, but it drove them to try nonetheless.

The term Hundred Schools of Thought is more of a nickname as there weren't exactly one hundred schools, How many we do not know but there were many. Some did dig into nature to discover its secrets, while many just were driven to find the strongest way to maintain a kingdom and make it stable.

After the Hundred Schools of Thought were founded. Emperor Qin Shi Huangdi unified China ending the warring States period bringing China into the Qin Dynasty. He has, for centuries, been decried as a barbarian who burned, persecuted and destroyed many of the other schools of thought at the time to make Legalism the state philosophy. This event is called The burning of books and burying of scholars as he supposedly buried 460 scholars alive.

However, modern scholars are now skeptical of this event as historian Sima Qian, centuries later in the Han dynasty around 100 years later, wrote the account that supposedly happened back in the Qin dynasty. Sima Qian ended up offending his emperor at the time who, instead of getting exiled, took castration as a punishment so that he had the ability to complete his encyclopedia. It is believed he used this story as a way to criticize the current anti-truth king without facing repercussions. So, more likely than not, the hundred schools declined as the major ones became the most popular, or merged with each other, ending in neglect. Not oppression.

We will begin discussing not the earliest but the most influential of the other Ru schools and we of course mean Confucius.

Confucianism

Kong-Fuzi, meaning master Kong, or the Latinized Confucius, is the most prominent and most well-known leader of a Ru school. His father was a commandant for a local lord and had a very weak royal lineage back to a duke in the Shang dynasty. His father died when Master Kong was 3, leaving them in poverty. Because his mother sacrificed for her son all of her life, Kong Qiu, as was his given name, was educated in a school for commoners where he learned the six arts of rites, music, archery, charioteering, calligraphy, and mathematics. These were skills that could move a common middle-class person into government positions. Because of this, and his minor royal status, he was able to spend his 20's in government jobs, such as bookkeeping.

His mother's sacrifice left a lasting

mark on him, who died young and in poverty, and was treated as the model mother in his works. Upon her death he spent 3 years away from public life in mourning, as was custom at the time, where he worked on perfecting his philosophy to allow anyone to be what he referred to as a Gentleman, who's bearing was the epitome of morality.

His teachings became well known among the Lu state where he served and was promoted to a governor of a minor town and later the minister of crime. The Duke of Lu made him his personal sage. The Duke had little power over the state but was instead run by 3 families under him called viscounts and ministers. Kong tried using diplomacy to help dismantle the power of three families and restore all power to the duke in the belief that the duke would be a great philosopher king similar to what Plato believed.

The Duke ended up not being the ideal person Kong thought he was, neglecting his duties to engage in pleasures of the flesh, and Kong decided to go into self-exile. He worked for the next 14 years, developing his philosophy and trying to discover a lord worthy of his services. He never succeeded in this second quest, each one leaving him disillusioned. However, he made a name for himself over China and eventually was

allowed to return to Lu where he spent his final 3-4 years teaching.

Kong Fuzi's philosophy

While Master Kong believed in an afterlife and astrology, as most did in his day, his philosophy discussed very little at all of the supernatural issues of the time. It was almost completely about virtues, ethics and how to live a good life so that society could be great. In some cases, he is considered a humanist, valuing human life over material possessions.

His philosophy was not based mostly on logic but more on stories of past people he deemed to be good and moral, especially rulers in mythic past.

He establish basically his version the golden rule of:

"What you do not wish for yourself, do not do to others."

Constant study was his creed to become a better person. Ignorance and naivety could lead to corruption, A generous action without sincerity was an empty gesture. Master Kong required constant diligence from his students to self-reflect and maintain perfect order of themselves not only in action but in thought. It is only by studying the past great people that one could learn to emulate them and become great people themselves. While doing something for one's own sake was not bad, if there is a choice between doing something for yourself or doing

something for all, the true gentleman would do it for all.

Ren are considered the 5 core values of Confucianism: Seriousness, generosity, sincerity, diligence and kindness. Confucius's moral system was based upon empathy and understanding others, rather than divinely ordained rules which most believed automatically made something right.
He was against legalism, thinking it did nothing to stop the root causes of corruption and evil.
"If the people are led by laws, and uniformity sought to be given to them by punishments, they will try to avoid the punishment, but have no sense of shame. If they are led by virtue, and uniformity sought to be given them by the rules of propriety, they will have the sense of shame, and moreover will become good."

He believed in a meritocracy but also that the mandate of heaven would unite all of China and a king would rule based on the merit of his morals and not from inherited lineage.

Every person should know their place and only rise by his own merit. Family loyalty and filial piety was the most important thing to him. Each member of the family had a natural pecking order and following the orders of a parent or elders were essential to be a good person.

While he wasn't successful at implementing his ideas in his lifetime, Confucianism became part of Chinese identity and was the ruling philosophy of many kings and lords. It found its way to neighboring nations. It was the top 3 philosophies that ruled China, alongside Taoism and Buddhism. Confucianism became one of the top schools to survive out of the hundred schools of thought. To this day it is considered the Number 1 State approved religion in China.

Mohism

Mo-tzu was born around the last years of Master Kong's life. His philosophy was more one of logic, rationality, and science, rather than ideals and throwbacks to golden age myths.
His philosophy preached impartial care, meaning having equal empathy for

everyone regardless of status or family bonds. He believed much of societal problems were caused not by a lack of empathy but that it was too concentrated and favoring certain socially prescribed people. He also believed that every person was equally deserving of material benefit and protection from harm. This was blasphemy to people who supported Confucius and some of the other schools of course.

There is something to this idea, as studies show that oxytocin, which is known for being the "love drug" in pop psychology, can increase altruism. But when altruism becomes ultra-concentrated in a small group, people become more distrustful of and bigoted against the out-group and people who are unlike them. This leads to nepotism and the ability to pit one group against another creating poverty and war.

Mohists set up networks of political advisors to spread their ideology. Mohism was much more a philosophy similar to modern utilitarianism and ignored old rituals and traditions when designing their moral systems. It prescribed that some traditions should be followed and some scrapped based on an outside objective observer system of morality. His utilitarianism was less toward pleasure and more toward order, material wealth of all and population growth, which at the time was needed to fight in armies and grow crops.

He believed that a government as

an organized unit can eliminate the inefficiency found in unorganized nature, which has some sound ideas in economies of scale where the larger the production, the less overhead costs there are. All rulers should surround themselves with honest and talented people, and while Mohism was not in favor of free speech for the commoners, honest communication by the civil servants, good and bad information from subjects to the leaders should be compulsory, as opposed to just telling the ruler what they want to hear out of fear. He also was against anything but self-defense when it came to violence and war.

His idea of impartial care, or equal empathy for all, spread to the government and was outspoken against nepotism, which modern governments also try to curb, and instead give the government jobs to the most qualified on a basis of merit. A ruler must base his decisions on the standard of heaven just as a carpenter does on his measuring tools, as heaven is the only perfection and the Law of Heaven is Love.

He preached a simple life for the leaders and the subjects. He believed many of the old rituals, such as massive funerals and expensive burials were very wasteful and the act of not wasting and simple living was much more noble and sacred. Mohism would be viewed in modern eyes as a philosophy of bureaucratic Hippies spreading meritocracy and love for all. Fatalism was another popular idea at the time that the Mohist rejected, the belief that the future was already written. Mozi believed this idea brought about starvation and suffering.

Aesthetics were useless and a waste of time to him, writing chapters against music and fine arts, indicating he did not understand how the human mind worked and how aesthetics could increase productivity and learning. However, his views on aesthetics were shaped by seeing Zhou rulers engaged in complex music and fine arts while their subjects starved to death. Had that art been spread to the masses he would have probably been able to see their value.

Mohism believed in truth no matter how good or how brutal, a foundation of

modern science as well as Buddhism. They focused on logic and mathematics and made some very important breakthroughs in these areas and their math made them perfect siege engineers at the time which they used for city defense and not offense.

Legalism

Legalism predated Confucianism in origin. The Legalists, or Fajia, did not so much care about morality or how society should be but instead took the latter purpose, discussing how to consolidate and stabilize power and autocratic authority for safety and stability. It is a school of thought often considered Machiavellian in the West. It had some Impact on both Confucianism and Taoism, as well as governing in modern China. It mentioned elements of inaction, or wuwei, which we will discuss later, but also had a brutal punishment but also a reward system prescribed by the government.

Legalism stressed a merit system much like the other schools of thought at the time, which led to the civil service exam, a grueling state exam where anyone could show their proficiency in ancient philosophy, great works, mathematics, poetry and other memorization requirements. If they passed, the man would get a lucrative government job, so villages would often pool their resources together to sponsor some of their most academically adept youth to take the exam, and in turn that new government employee would send money back to their village as gratitude. It was one of the few ways a poor person had upward mobility in China.

Shen Buhai is credited with having had a lot of impacts on Fajia, and its political reforms in the Qin state, allowing it to become a military power, which allowed Emperor Qin Shi Huangdi to unify China. Shen penned the Han Feizi, a cornerstone of Legalism and had a big impact on both the Tao Te Ching and Sun Tzu's art of war.

Unlike the Confucius' Gentleman or philosopher king, The Fujia prince ruled through appearance and perception. He surrounds himself with an Aura of Wei(majesty), shi(authority, influence) and uses shu, or the art of political stagecraft. Using this collective power or Fa(administrative methods and standards) along with a competent merit-based bureaucracy, a ruler can rule the nation not from benevolence, righteousness, reason or ability but subdues purely through Fa to become absolute ruler and restore the world. By modern standards, this is very close to fascism. Aristocrats also would rely on Fa to control their local subordinates.

It was like feudalism but with some tweaks. It cared not about individual's opinions but believed that with a strong leader, the majority would benefit.

After the Qin empire, Fajia lost prominence for its rather brutal punishment system, though it left its mark indefinitely on

Shen Buhai influential founder of Legalism

151

Emperor Qin Shi Huangdi who united China under Legalism

China as the Chinese governments continued its systems. It rose and fell throughout the rest of history, including the Ming and even to a small extent, modern Communist China.

The School of Yin-Yang or the Naturalists

This school invented the Yin-Yang and later the Chinese 5 elements that are essential to Feng Shui and Traditional Chinese medicine. Much of their works were lost or were absorbed into Taoism. Yin Yang is the idea that all of reality is part of a whole and extremes are two sides of the same coin. Yin represents dark, cold, female, and negative, while yang represents light, hot, male, and positive. Everything has a yin or yang counterpart. The 5 elements, on the other hand, exploit a unique property of odd numbers. If you take all 5 elements of earth, fire water, wood and metal, put them in a circle, then draw a 5-pointed star between them and arrows pointed between each point, you can have a perfect check and balance system.

One element harms the other, one element strengthens another. A very similar way the number three is used for rock, paper, scissors and the 3 branches of government in the US. It was a method of achieving homeostasis and many believed that using signals from the body or their surrounding environment, a lack of a certain element could be helped or too much of an element could be harmed through artificial means

Bragnir and Frodhi Demonstrate the principle of Yin Yang

in the body. From this school you get the beginning of traditional Chinese medicine, which involves eating certain foods or herbs strong in a certain element, to balance the elements in your body. Every herb and food was classified by what element they belonged to.

The Naturalists were also responsible for Feng Shui, a complex geomancy, which they believed could help fix your luck based on positioning and placement of items around you to balance the elements. Much of it is just mindful placement and maintaining a clean and tidy environment along with aesthetics to lift the spirit, however people would take it so far as to knock down entire wings of their houses because they didn't have the right feng shui positioning.

The Naturalists were some of the first to begin experimenting in nature, and

probably influenced some of the alchemists that helped Emperor Qin Shi Huangdi. These were also potentially responsible for the Emperor's death. Sima Qian claimed that Emperor Qin was so obsessed with immortality that he tried many alchemist's potions and died of poisoning.. This too may be a mocking insult of the contemporary king by Sima Qian and Emperor Qin may

153

have died from something entirely different. From these alchemists, the Chinese discovered one of their 4 greatest inventions, gunpowder, the other three being paper, the first printing press and the compass which would change the world even more.

This school was absorbed by the religious wing of Taoism that went on to impact China for millennia.

The School of Names or the Logicians

This school was essentially a school of sophists and was discussed very disparagingly by later Mohists, Taoists and Confuscionists. The school was initially a branch

Gongsun Long, of the school of names

that grew out of the Mohist school. Nearly all of their works are lost so we only have their opponents' points of view to go on and not their own. According to their detractors, this was a school that taught you how to win any argument using purely debate tactics and cherry picking the facts that support your claim while doing everything you could to have people ignore or not think about any of the counter arguments.

Mohists hated these people who they claimed hacked people's logic and good nature for their own benefit. Modern scam artists and internet trolls rely on this method and understanding their tactics is essential to saving yourself from getting tricked or stuck in a pointless argument that you can never win because the point was never about finding the truth but about winning the argument only by injecting doubt and distorting the evidence. According to the few lines we have from them, they appear to possibly have something akin to Zeno's paradox, and were perhaps closer to the Greek philosophers than any other branch of Chinese philosophy.

Many more schools of thought are both known and unknown but fell out of favor at the time, either being absorbed by or muscled out by the bigger names. Now armed with this knowledge, we will move forward to the main subject of this section, Taoism.

The School of Taoism

　　*Taoism as a philosophy is different from the religion, at least to the Western mind. The religion of Taoism is an animistic ancestor worshiping traditional religion, very much akin to Shinto in Japan. It has gods and demons and an afterlife. Divination such as the I Ching, traditional Chinese medicine, and Feng Shui which is a form of geomancy. The Tao, or Dao as it's pronounced, just means "the way." The way involves living in harmony with nature and understanding it more for a better life.

　　While here in the West we distinguish the philosophy and the religion as separate, some believe that this is a Western Protestant view and not really a thing the people of China distinguish as being different. It's been proposed that the idea came about from protestant missionaries who were seeing the religion through their own biased lenses and seeing Taoism, the religion, as akin to Catholicism with all of their extra non-canonical additions to the belief. Taoism, the philosophy, however, was viewed much more like the Protestant church who used the bible only to base the religion on and was a much more pure version. The Tao Te Ching, the Chuang Tzu and the Leihtzi being the true version and the religion a corruption of the pure form.

　　That said, just like how we must separate Buddhism from its religious supernatural elements for this discussion to just

155

its philosophical roots, we must do the same here with Taoism, as the supernatural is by definition not testable or provable by science, so dropping all of that out just leaves us with the traditionally Western-defined philosophy of the Tao.

The philosophy of Taoism was said to be written by a wise old man named Lao Tzu, (which just means old master). He was said to be old at the time of Confucius, but the works attributed to Master Lao appear to have come after the rise of Confucius and as a reaction to their strict teachings, which leads scholars to believe that he was a literary figure and not a real person. The fact that his name describes what he is, is a usual sign that someone is a myth.

His book the Tao Te Ching is said to have been written when Lao Tzu essentially gave up on society and left to go live as a hermit in nature. The gatekeeper at the frontier who was a devoted follower of Master Lao refused to let him pass his gate until he wrote down his teaching for future generations. Master Lao agreed, amicably but also grumpily, and wrote the book of 81 short chapters, and then went off into the wilderness, never to be seen again.

That's a nice story, but academic research traces each chapter of the Tao Te Ching to have been written by different Taoist thinkers over about a 100 year period, adding to the belief that Master Lao never existed but their use of him created a

mythical figure that acted perfectly in step with the Tao that people could try and replicate.

Master Lao didn't actively teach much of anything. He lived it. In mostly silence. And his supposed disciples followed him to observe him and how he acted and lived, in sync with the Tao. Learning to be more aware of the reality around them, more observation, less action and speech, so that when they did act or speak, they would make a much bigger impact than if they acted or spoke all the time and did not observe.

Science is quite similar. If there is a drug in testing that shows promise, many wish the scientists would let them try the drug in case it works. If it turns out to be "the cure" they would benefit from it. However, without sufficient observation, trying any drug in the observation process could most easily lead to a waste of money for that person they probably don't have, and at worst, have long term negative health impacts or death. It must go through certain levels of testing and observation first before it can be used so it can have the most impact with the least harm.

Lack of observation and awareness can cause harm, even when the intentions are the best in the world. Some of the worst atrocities are made possible by harnessing some of the best human emotional impulses, but with some of the worst understanding of reality. Much like how someone with

schizophrenia suffers from hallucinations, if what they were experiencing was true, their reactions would be completely logical and rational. Instead, they often end up hurting themselves, others or property because their hallucination gives them a completely

incorrect view of reality, and when they come out of the episode, they find they have broken something they sometimes cannot undo without proper support and care.

It was said that for ninety years, Lao refused to write or say anything, believing that truth cannot be taught. There is some truth that words and the human language are limited. They cannot ever fully describe anything, as there is too much to know about anything. Also the human mind is

too limited to hold all of those facts and all of that information. People who think they understand a country they are excited to visit, no matter what, will have some form of culture shock when they get there. Even the most researched person still experiences a dramatic break in their reality when they actually visit a country. I don't know how many people I've talked to who were excited because they were visiting America, and they visited some place like Indiana. It is 100% part of America but when foreigners

hear America, they think Hollywood movies and City glamor. Big architectural feats and monuments. That is "Real" America. Not cookie-cutter houses, sleepy towns, and no night life. Politicians, on the other hand,

over the past decade have equated small towns with "Real" America, the polar opposite to what foreigners view as "Real" America..

Both are right. America is rural and urban, large city AND small towns, high-paced, exciting, flashy and slow-paced, humble, and laid back. Both have benefits and drawbacks.

Every scientific law has an exception, every scientific definition is leaving out things the user often knows but the receiver may not. When going to a different country, something as simple as road signs, manhole cover designs, food packaging, or a social

faux pas will throw you no matter how much time you've spent on the internet studying it, and even that differs from region to region in each nation.

Master Lao

It is said that Master Lao would always go for walks in silence and his neighbors would follow in silence. "Hello" and small talk were not permitted, as they were meaningless. Once a visitor wanted to come along, he didn't understand how to deal with the silence, and it became crushing. Talking and words often are used to distract yourself and prevent you from being unstimulated and bored. Remember the shock experiment discussed in the segment on Zen?

Boredom in psychological terms is linked to disgust. This acts as a great mover from a biological point of view, but we also have the cerebral cortex that needs time alone to think and come up with the best method of attack on life. I would always tell my students as an adjunct instructor that boredom is the muscle soreness you feel when you are working out, but with your mind. If you can force your way through it, you can be mentally stronger and smarter.

In Herman Hess's Siddhartha he said, "If I can think, I can meditate, and I can fast. I can do anything." There is some truth to this. If you can do without and you can do just fine without outside stimulus, you are at an advantage over other people who must consume and must be stimulated. Some neurological disorders make this impossible for some people like extreme ADHD but even then, meditation can be helpful.

Interestingly, this book's protagonist went from materialistic, to aesthetic to Buddhist, back to materialistic and ended up essentially a Taoist finally in his life even if there was no real word for it in the book.

Words can also be used to hide your real life and real situation. You do this all the time at work where no one wants to know what is really going on or what you believe.

That could cause divisions and animosity. You use small talk as a bridge to mask your true self and put on a front. To some idealists this sounds very fake, but it acts as social lubricant to ensure people who may hate each other's views can get along and work toward a single goal. Unlike what the Taoists believe, because we were always tribal creatures and not solitary individuals like tigers, we developed this small talk to ensure tribal cohesion. Group consensus was needed even if the consensus was wrong, if it moved the group together, things tended to work more often than not through the wisdom of the crowd.

That said, when you have the ability to self-reflect and observe, words often get in the way and create a smoke screen, preventing you from seeing the truth about yourself. Constantly defining is essential for some things and it's not real to your logical mind

159

until it's defined. This can have merit, but it can also be a hindrance if you unknowingly use it wrong, just moving you further from understanding your situation. Often by defining something you stick it into a category that you create a comparison to better understand it in a more simplified way like a metaphor or an analogy. However, if you aren't careful, you can assume other comparisons between the analogy and reality that are not true and break the metaphor's usefulness without realizing it, creating an unknown biased falsehood.

With Master Lao and the poor visitor, the silence was so awkward and made him feel so naked that he was embarrassed. So, he said, "What a beautiful sun. Look…! What a beautiful sun is born! What a beautiful morning!" This was all he said and no one else said a word, so he shut up.

The next day, Master Lao told the visitor's friend, "Don't bring that man, he talks too much. He speaks uselessly. I have eyes and can see it is a beautiful sun and is being born. Why say it?"

To Master Lao, saying something was beautiful destroyed the beauty and wonder of the thing because turning it into words destroyed the experience that is much more important than words. There is some truth to this in the fact that a study by Linda Henkel that has been replicated twice in the last decade has shown that if you take a picture of something, you remember it less clearly than if you experience it for what it is without trying to record it to watch or view later. The act of trying to capture it makes the experience much weaker in your own mind, meaning you haven't truly experienced it in full as a whole if you try to capture or define an experience and while you can go back and watch or think about the experience there are so many pieces missing, such as your emotional reactions to it, the smells, the motion, the size and scale.

Goodness is natural

*The central belief of Taoism is that society, laws, and industry make people unethical. Being one with nature by following its rules makes it impossible to be unethical. To be truly ethical, you must drop all of the rules you know and follow the Tao and you will know what is good and ethical as second nature. It is the creation of rules that forces people to break them and be unethical. It is nurture not nature that makes us evil and our environment makes us bad. Civilization is unnatural. You don't need to find wisdom, you already have it. It's just been suppressed by civilization and rules.

There is something to this idea as our industrial-minded work and learning system often goes against the way we evolved. If we can change the environment to better go with the flow of how we evolved, we can be more efficient. Things like getting more sleep and more time off work actually increases

160

productively but the protestant work ethic in the states goes against this and companies believe they can squeeze more work out of people by letting them take less time off. It's laziness to have so much paid time off, while labor science shows that the less rested people are, the more people mess up at work, who then spend that time trying to correct the errors. If they just got plenty of rest and time off, they would skip that mess up in the first place and have more free time and rest, they can be slightly more productive and efficient than the time lost.

Germany and Belgium are just as productive as the US, but we work 40-60 hours a week, and they have 6 weeks paid vacation and 37-hour work weeks that they stick to religiously. Often the person isn't bad, the environment just goes against the way we evolved, making being good and productive much harder than it should be.

Sadly, unless you have the science to study human behavior, you often won't understand the way humans actually behave in their environment and as science is often counter intuitive, one will do the opposite of what is reality and wonder why they get bad results. It must be the inherent evil of humans.

Surrendering to nature

When Lao left for his death at 90 years of age, he believed he was going back into nature, the original source. Pure, lonely and uncontaminated by human civilization. While Taoists had a belief in returning to an untouched pure form of nature, any place the human species has touched, they have changed and augmented it in some way, even the most "untouched" pristine area. We will stop natural fires from starting, which will cause too much growth and create massive fires. The Amazon rainforest and the island of Japan are much more fertile than they should be as humans mulched the Amazon with coconut shells, and the Japanese brought sheep and goats to japan and their waste turned the scrubland into a lush place to grow crops.

Native peoples would burn the American forestlands, spreading the prairies and grasslands so that deer and bison could roam and graze unhindered making up for their lack of domesticable livestock. They also domesticated areas where wild berries and other edible plants grew in forests, which shaped what we think as "naturally abundant" forests today. It worked well as Cahokia had more inhabitants than London did when it existed. When Europeans came, the diseases they brought wiped out 90- 95% of the population. There was not enough to maintain burning so trees grew up everywhere, most of them grew too close together because they didn't have an established canopy like old forests that prevent them from crowding each other. 50 years later, settlers landed and had no idea that this mess of

forest was actually very unnatural, but believed it was, as they referred to it, "untrammeled" wilderness.

Thousands of years of burning and animal fertilizing made the soil insanely nutrient rich and great for crops, farming, and ranching compared with Europe until modern fertilization science took off. In medieval Europe, all woods and forest were altered in some way and treated more as an orchard for fruit or lumbering, or in cases of some trees, cut specifically while they were growing so they would grow staves for barrel making. Most American state Parks we think of as the symbols of nature are land stolen from native people so white people could go someplace to enjoy what they viewed as untouched nature. Humans are nature too.

We have touched and changed everything. Even Mount Everest is now polluted with dead bodies and human feces. Antarctica now has records of air pollution levels in its ice cores and researchers studying them find lead put into the air during the Roman and Chinese empires.

Humans should not try to find nature, we are nature. What we need and desire to our core is beauty and clean air and water. That is what a wooded hike allows for. Fresh air purified by the trees, certain soil microbes getting into your nose and releasing dopamine, time to think in silence and listen to the forest sounds, even if the place was altered and crafted by humans for your enjoyment.

"Surrendering to Nature" as an ideal,

even during Lao's time was no longer fully possible, even if they tried to return to a hunter/gatherer lifestyle they had long since forgotten. However, learning to understand nature and work with it as we are part of it is the closest one can reach and is much better for everyone who embraces it.

Truth is silence

There is something to the belief that truth can only be found through silence. It is when you are alone that you can allow your reflective brain to roam. With the noise of interactions, you are reactive, and you represent what you have cultivated during your reflective time. True understanding and learning requires a period of time to just sit and think about the idea. Training yourself requires some alone time, away from distractions. Some people feel that they can focus more when loud music or TV background noise is playing because that creates artificial silence for them, especially if parts of their brain are easily distracted. Music has some ability to make you push further and give you more drive to do something hard or boring.

However, taking silence to the extreme that Lao Tzu did may actually be counterproductive. Mind you, if he was a literary creation to be the ideal of something, that would make sense. He embodies Tao, which is silence. Then again, without experiencing social interactions, you face a false sense of reality.

In my period where I felt like I was "enlightened," I was also incredibly anti-social. This isolated me. The human brain, no matter how much we enjoy being alone, demands social interaction on some level for good mental health. I of course was unable to be social because I had none of the tools to do so, as someone on the Autism Spectrum.

Henry David Thoreau was one of the first Westerners to idealize solitude, even though by modern standards he wasn't isolated at all and his mom and many other people came by. What he considered solitude is now called just "Me time," a time to relax the mind and not have to socialize. That could mean meditation, reading, having a think like Pooh, or just binging TV. This concept was completely novel to people in the past. Being antisocial was impossible as you were constantly working with people and relied on making social inroads to better your status among the tribe or group. Failure to do this could end in your death.

Modern technology has allowed us to be alone, but it has gone to the extreme where we are isolated on an unhealthy level of atomized individuality and the brain still craves human interaction even if people bug the crap out of us because that is how we evolved to be. It is why solitary confinement is torture. I always assumed that if I was in prison for some reason, I would prefer to go to solitary to protect myself from inmates, but the brain starts going crazy and twisted and hallucinating if you spend too long alone. .

That said, the Ru who wrote and invented Master Lao probably were some of the few who had time and wealth to reflect and be alone. They saw its value, this rare beautiful thing that was so scarce, so they assumed all of it must be good. Similar to how a fat venus figurine was viewed as a great thing because they aren't hungry, no one at the time had the luxury except for the doctors of the very wealthy to know the dangers and side effects of going in the opposite direction with isolation, with body fat and inactivity. Gautama Siddharta would have said to take the middle path on this and have

plenty of time to be social and plenty of time to be alone so you can feed the reflective and reactive self. As a person on the spectrum, I have a much harder time giving up my desire to be alone and forcing myself to be social to be in balance and I have to actively work to feed that practice of socializing or I can be somewhat annoying when I haven't had enough practice.

Lao Tzu claimed that the Tao is a lonely path as people don't want to see or know the truth. I certainly felt like that growing up, but the older I get and the more connected we are, the more I find that is less true. Having everyone agree with you is a lonely path but the truth is difficult to come by and can require us to be jarred by the people around us to realize that we were

actually the ones deluded about something. So long as you are with people who are also actively seeking truth, the Tao is not lonely at all, the silence may feel lonely but to someone of his time, it must have been so hard to find people even remotely interested in discovering the truth and socializing.

If you only reflect, you never know if what you reflected on holds up in practice and you can delude yourself. You must experiment with your ideas to find out if they are true by jumping into society. At the other extreme, if you don't have enough reflective time, it's hard to learn, hard to change yourself, hard to keep track of who and what is true. You have to rely more on the hive mind instead of thinking for yourself. This is also a yin and a yang. Master Lao is possibly unknowingly breaking his own rules of being in balance because his creators couldn't imagine that being an issue.

The Tao can only be experienced.

The Tao cannot be said with words, the full truth cannot be said. But it can give enough of an approximate for a specific situation and system. It can also, over time, like waves on a rock, nudge you toward the understanding of how to find the truth or at least the truth you need at that time. The whole truth is too big, or we would have a unified theory model by now. Our perceptions are limited, as Richard Dawkins put it. We are but looking through a slit in the blackness of ignorance and getting a peak at part of reality.

A combined logical fallacy used is that "because you don't have an answer and I do, my answer must be right." This is a mix of a false dichotomy and an argument from ignorance fallacy. This idea hinges on the brain's natural bias for the need for closure, because not knowing sits uncomfortably with us. When dealing with science, you are surrounded by unknowns and it is very noble to say "I don't know" when you simply don't. It's just this blank hollow uncertainty that we have slowly been tearing open as a species with better understanding all the time, but we must learn to sit in silence

and be ok with not knowing and not filling it with an answer just because it's an answer. And even with an answer or potential answer, you must ensure it's not fixed too strongly as science has a way of upending fixed facts, though very rarely entire theories which are complex explanations for collections of facts that have so much evidence it would take an insurmountable number of facts to overturn it that we can view it as close to certain as you can get.

For many philosophers, the idea that truth cannot be said with words hinges on the idea that truth is an experience, but even that is a lie, it is partial truth. You could be hallucinating. It's a natural part of being a human and more common than you might

think. You had an experience, but is it the truth? Maybe. Since we all have different experiences, division of labor and division of knowledge, in science we bypass the parochial effect and confer with each other, especially with someone who is an impartial observer to determine if the experience is real.

Sometimes you had a random one off. Your brain sees patterns and takes note of that, even though statistically there is nothing special about your experience and

it was bound to happen. Before believing it has some significant meaning outside of the statistical mundane You will want your ideas and experiences to have as many knowledgeable eyes looking at it to counter your own biases. This phenomena may not be the norm or it may be statistically predictable, or something about you could make it pretty unlikely that you experienced a certain reality no matter how real it felt.

For people suffering from depression, one of the things they are taught is to ask themselves, "is it possible that this reality is real but not true?" Perhaps while I do feel like a complete piece of scum, the world is too awful for words and everyone else around me would be better off if I was dead, maybe this thought is real but my perception is warped and not actually true. Maybe people would be way worse off if you died and maybe you are actually just as good as most people, you just are comparing yourself to an image you have or others that is false. Or maybe because your dopamine and serotonin levels are too low you are seeing the world with darkened lenses like Dorthy in the Emerald city, the city isn't actually emerald, the glasses just made you believe it was.

Let's take the idea of love, as another example. Many will say that love cannot be expressed with words but experience. That is true, but it can be classified due to careful outside observation. Love, in the English language, has so many meanings that it is nearly meaningless. It could be brotherly love, parental love, erotic love or infatuation, a commitment to work as hard as possible to stick together and work on your relationship, or a self-love to move on from a relationship with a person who you are mismatched with. All of these are love. All of these can only be experienced but it is only often in hindsight that you have the down time and can see through your emotions to classify and determine what type of love it was or to see if that wasn't really love and better learn how to find actual love.

When learning the Tao, there is no need for a teacher because he can't say anything to you in words to make you fully understand the Tao. The teacher can only deprogram you of society. There is no technique for learning about the Tao. Technique goes against the Tao because you are not looking for an outcome, you are just existing in time. You have to unlearn your conditioning, and once you do that, you can experience the Tao.

Taoism often denigrates education, and intellectuals. Much of this is because all ancient Chinese education involved purely memorization which gave people merit and made themselves think they were wise. In the modern world the best education relies only on enough memorization to recognize patterns and train the brain to be capable of memorizing. After that it involves the ability to think, observe, control oneself from making logical fallacies and harness one's creativity and observation. Once these are established, quite often the brain then seeks and desires new knowledge and self-improvement as opposed to forcing oneself to memorize, which would often lead to being unable to come up with a thought for oneself in the future with the desire for learning effectively dead.

You must work hard to your utmost to aim for enlightenment until the hard work becomes a barrier to enlightenment. Once that occurs then you have to drop your effort and stop trying. An amature artist or archer doesn't become one until they have worked themselves to the point that they lose themselves in the work and then they transform into an artist. After a certain point, often it becomes such second nature that you can no longer explain things to a layperson because you cannot understand what they don't know and many feel they have better things to do than to spend time listening to

discover what they don't understand.

This makes for a terrible teacher sadly. The science community is terrible at this. People who never struggled with learning science are often terrible at explaining it. Pretty much every field can be explained by breaking it down to its smaller parts and if the instructor doesn't care enough or doesn't have the time to listen, to discover the flaws in one's understanding, it will be impossible for people to learn. I have found when most people appear to not understand something, they actually can understand and can grasp the majority of a subject. However, when there are small flaws in their knowledge, from that point onward everything about their understanding is wrong and warped by the flaw, or is extra difficult for them to understand.

Taoism "hates education" because it hated the education system at the time of its inception. There are great modern education systems that work along the lines of Taoist teachers. Ancient Taoists would be blown away by some of our modern institutions. That is not to say that most of them would pass this so-called Taoist test. While many, especially for poorer students, still rely on memorization over everything else, hopefully someday education in general will include all the things mentioned so far in this book to ensure people are much less gullible and more in tune with reality, nature, and naturally evolved psychology.

The Biases and Science

Science requires a clear understanding of bias to ensure they don't bring their own into their research. It has happened too many times in the past and to this day we are finding old studies retested now with controls for biases that are not able to be replicated. For most of the early 1900s, there were no or few controls for bias in science leading to so many bad or unreproducible studies that in hindsight turned out to be a waste of time and resources.

Belief, decision-making and behavioral biases.

Confirmation bias is a selective search of information which means that you will read, notice or select only information that backs up your beliefs. Many times you will accept sources from a person or brand name, because at one point you tended to agree with the logic of that source or felt the source type to be true. If the accuracy changes, you may accept something new that is massively flawed because it's from that source. In science, we should always take scientific papers in our field with a grain of salt until we have analyzed them for ourselves and listened to other experts who may have contradictory arguments, otherwise known as peer reviewed.

When a scientist argues against the merits of a paper, many times one can view that scientist as just being "mean" because that study and possible discovery was a lot of work. It gives pseudo-scientists the

appearance of some credibility when they claim signs of persecution because all their papers are rejected. However, because of the feeling of knowing, there must be independent analyzers with no emotional attachment to the idea to chew it over logically before accepting it. A scientist must keep that doubt in his or her mind and realize that we can never be 100% gnostic about science but we can strive to be pretty close when we have piles of evidence from repeated data sampling or experimentation and when the scientific consensus agrees on something and just a tiny fraction of scientists disagree. Leaving that door of doubt cracked open makes it much easier to change your mind if someone else discovers something to overturn the currently held theory.

There will be detractors in science through confirmation bias. I would personally like to not believe anthropogenic or man-made climate change is real, but there is too much evidence for it. There is a very tiny minority of scientists that still believe it is not man made by reading only evidence they want to believe. These are people either not in the field with time and energy to put into filtering all the evidence, or they are bad scientists often paid by corporations for their air of expertise and legitimacy, only selecting the data that confirms their belief, cementing another false bias.

Erik von Danican, the writer of "Ancient Astronauts," a book claiming

169

humans were genetically modified by aliens and every religious text is true but describing aliens, directly admitted to only pointing out facts that back up his theory and didn't see anything wrong with that.

Let's go back to music and biases. Another version of this bias is when a person listens to a new song by an artist they already like. The person will more likely give that artist a free pass on a song, even if the song is subpar, while being much more critical of an artist they dislike, even if the song fits everything they enjoy in a music.

Many times, people do not like new songs or certain styles of music. Initially. However, if people mentally link the music with positive or nostalgic experiences, they can love a song even if before they thought it "sucked." Music companies know this and will attempt to insert music they want to sell into every aspect of life that they can.

One of the big causes of the rise of the popularity of modern corporate hip-hop and R&B can be linked back to an illegal deal with record producers and radio stations to play more corporately produced hip-hop and less small-time local bands and artists. This linked more "good" memories with the product and also produced the illusion that it was very popular. The lie became the truth as society and tastes changed to fit the new music genre. This is known in psychology as the **Mere Exposure effect**, which is simply defined as the more one sees something, the more normalized it is and normalized things are comforting. The Mona Lisa was considered one of Da Vinci's least important works compared to say The Lady with an Ermine, but an art heist in in the 1920's splashed the picture all over the papers and people now consider it one of his best pieces mostly because it's the one they are most familiar with.

There are biases where we have a strong desire to put more meaning on things that aren't there. We find patterns in places where there are none. This bias is called **Pareidolia**. This is wired into us and many species. If we can find a pattern in what appears to be a confused mess, it makes life so much easier. We can do things mindlessly. Mindfulness is at the core of Buddhism and Taoism and these biases are the enemies of awareness and the way. Digging through your own acquired beliefs and realizing you are being mindless is a lifelong practice, especially if those mindless ideas are not challenged.

In the case of a tragedy, especially a random senseless one, the brain tries to find patterns and make sense of it because it needs an explanation often with some agency. In the Abrahamic faiths it is easier to rationalize it as the will of God, or in some cases, the work of Satan. Barring that, the brain can go into conspiracy mode, and the bigger the profile, the more likely a conspiracy theory would come from it.

The Kennedy assassination from government records mandatorily released 50 years after the incident showed no highly organized killing, just a mix of luck on the part of the gunman and lapses in security protocol. But people jumped onto every single conspiracy theory they could from the Illuminati to J. Edgar Hoover all the way to the communists or bankers trying to prevent change back to the gold standard. There was a small coverup to protect one of the secret service agents and his family for making a mistake in the process from being persecuted and harassed and that was enough to raise suspicions that it all was a highly orchestrated plot and coverup.

The same is true about 9/11. Both were senseless tragedies that made people feel helpless. People hate feeling helpless, so their brain makes up reasons for it no matter how crazy or irrational, or in the case of the widow and the Buddha, the belief that the universe will change its laws just for you because somehow you are special. I know that in moments of grief and denial and pleading I have hoped for or even believed a miracle could occur, especially during my religious period. The reality is sobering and painful but not accepting it and resisting just makes the pain worse because on top of the strain of dealing with the grief, you also have the stress of trying to deny it is happening.

Belief Bias and Framing

Biased interpretation of information relies on more rationalization. Harsh standards for evidence that goes against your view and weaker standards for evidence that

goes toward your view. Many times you will give more scrutiny to someone or a source you dislike or normally disagree with and give a free pass to something you agree with and repeat word of mouth or unstudied concepts as "facts" because you heard it from someone you trust. There has been a decline in belief among the public in terms of anthropogenic climate change, especially in the US. You can see this divide at work even in prejudice and cognitive biases developed across political lines.

People in the Republican party speak out against anthropogenic climate change mostly because their perceived enemies, the Democrats, accept it. Couple this further with American media that has created a level of distrust of the intelligentsia. If a person

avoids terms people are taught to distrust, such as "evolution" or "global warming" and just lays out facts using other words, or in an appearance that doesn't sound "sciency," many times one can be convinced of evolution and climate change as they haven't shut down their brain from listening to evidence the second you say the feared buzzed words.

The essentials of PR and advertising are to say things that may not be logical fallacies themselves but instead use psychology that will encourage people who are not aware of logical fallacies and have not trained themselves to avoid them, to make their own. This is called framing, and it's studied in communications and rhetoric in depth. If you can frame the debate, then it ensures that you can argue the points you want and ignore other points that might be relevant. If you start out advertising an insult toward your opponent, it emotionally nudges the person to be biased against that other person. It leads people to assume the **ad hominem** logical fallacy even if you aren't bringing that other argument into the discussion. This fallacy is essentially "this person did a bad thing and is therefore wrong on something else too". .

Anti-politically correct types also tend to hate PC-types for the reason that being PC can cause a viewer to make an appeal to authority, or follow the fallacy of the **wisdom of repugnance**, which is when a person discusses something gross or taboo and sees it as automatically bad. The only way to counter framing is by being aware of it and learning how to change the frame yourself, avoiding language used by the framer, and creating your own new language to create your own frame.

Framing at its most powerful involves taking complex concepts and metaphors that are well known to the public and using them as analogies to imply other things. An analogy is just a comparison and while very useful to increasing understanding under limited conditions, it works to a certain point and after that breaks down. But a dishonest framer, who understands implications and the language of the audience, can push the analogy a little further than it should ever go and imply a lot more in favor

of their position than it should ever logically merit.

George Lakeoff, who wrote Don't think about an Elephant (2004), is one of the foremost scholars on framing and how the GOP used it to change the way people categorized ideas. They were able to take the complex concepts of mother and father and apply them dishonestly to the two political parties. Democrats were mothers, who, from a democrat's perspective, doesn't sound that bad. Mothers are caring. They want to help, they want to heal, and they work super hard to raise good kids. But the GOP was able to twist that dichotomy and move mothers to mean weak, coddling, overbearing, soft, and unrealistic, while it is us, the Republicans, the fathers that are strong, realistic, disciplinarians, use tough love, are the real hard workers and who made big changes occur. We are the ones who know what's really going on. Not the soft, lesser intelligent, over emotional women.

This dishonest framing worked really well. They took complex metaphors and analogies and pushed them past their breaking points while shutting down alternative views of how these analogies could be taken, shutting down all dialogue. Democrats were run roughshod over for decades, always on the defensive and most often ignorant as to why their ideas weren't resonating when they worked in the past.

David Frum was one of the most

well-known GOP political operatives who helped George W Bush get elected by literally having a polling survey company ask people what their opinions about certain words were and what emotional responses they triggered and then had the correct words used in speeches to trigger those emotional responses. This was how Bush was able to do things other politicians may have not gotten away with.

Language changes. Societal feelings towards language changes over the years and this approach would be very expensive to maintain, which leads to another insidious point. Those with money are able to do it way more than small political groups, meaning that people absorb those messages much better than the messages of groups that fail to use this kind of framing. Those with money hold power and shape the framing by exploiting biases.

It doesn't mean they have better ideas, in fact often they have worse ideas or corrupt ideas, but it means they are better salesmen and can convince people they have the better idea and that often is way more important than being actually correct.

The social biases

Evaluation apprehension is when the brain is required to make a judgment with real world implications and repercussions, which if given sufficient time reduces the **primacy effect** and other biases, but having time pressure increases the power of these biases even more so. This time pressure creates an artificial situation called the "**need for cognitive closure**," as we discussed in the section on Buddhism, where any answer is better emotionally than ambiguity and confusion. The brain will do what is called, "seizing and freezing," where it will latch onto all of the first information it takes in and lock down their assessment of the situation immediately as more information would cause more confusion thereby causing stress.

One of the major probable mechanisms behind this phenomenon is that the limbic or emotional animal brain remembers things for a very long time, while the neocortex or logical human brain does not remember nearly as well because it has to focus on and filter through so many details. At the beginning, the limbic system attaches an emotion to the person and then holds that emotion even while the neocortex is analyzing the facts. It's also quite possibly where most superstitions came from as the limbic system tied whatever you were doing with either positive or negative effects and even though your neo-cortex could logically deduce that it is a random effect, your limbic system is stronger and you could convince yourself using logic that it was effective.

This does have an evolutionary advantage back in the days where finding a mate involved picking one out of a group based on certain tells and signs. They often didn't have time and energy to be selective and choosy or they would lose out. Our tribal evolution didn't weed this trait out either as we probably knew everyone in our tribe fairly in depth before we decided to mate with them, and our us vs them mindset helped maintain the solitude. Captured or transferred new members of the tribe took time to get integrated and figure out the social system. Depending on the tribe, they may have never been truly accepted but acceptance wasn't required for sex and sexual attraction to occur.

This is why when a young man or woman talks down about themselves, they may think they are just being open and honest, but the brain of the person they are interested in won't register it as such, making a quick judgment call, and any positive thing the person has going for them will be automatically dismissed by the person they are trying to pursue because it doesn't fit into their certainty based definition of that person.

One of the things that the brain can do to maintain a feeling of knowing is to swap the order of events that caused the brain to believe something. If you wish to be accepted into a group that believes in something or likes something, your brain can swap the events that caused it to like or believe what you believe. You can believe you believed or liked something independently

and your friends happened to believe or think that also. This is called the **Bandwagon effect** which is the belief that one comes up with an idea independently to hide it from themselves that they came up with the idea for emotional reasons such as acceptance, rebellion or agreement and not logic.
Memory bias

When you see a scientist in a movie claim that all their notes are "up here" and points at their brain, they are a bad scientist. Movies like to portray a scientific genius as one with total recall and before we understood the mind and memory biases we believed these were the case, however, one bias-type science has down pat in never having an issue with is memory bias just through good note-taking and proper citation. So much bad data would be generated if the scientist relied on their memory.

One of the worst biases that would plague them would be the **Generated Effect Bias** also called the self-generated effect bias, where one remembers things one created better than one created by others. So if a scientist comes up with a brilliant sounding idea they could easily spout it over and over again as fact, without having to back it up. Some of the worst charlatans who believe their own bad ideas suffer from this as their ego gets so badly in the way. If they actually had to back up their claims with sources of every little piece of their idea, their lovely idea might fall apart. Or if they had to show their work and their notes or blind themselves from the data while crunching the statistics for the experiments they claim they did, they might show lots of bad errors in their memory or how they screw the data based on their own ego. These are the people most likely to claim persecution by the scientific community because if you can't even properly show your work in the scientific note taking and citation process there is a good chance your memories and biases are going to get in the way.

Leveling and Sharpening Bias is where Memory distortions are introduced by the loss of details in our memory over time, often caused by our sharpening or selective recollection of certain details that take on exaggerated significance in relation to the details or aspects of the experience that is lost through leveling. Both biases may be reinforced over time, and by repeated recollection or re-telling of a memory. Just like with the Challenger study, our memories are rewritten every time we recall it and every single time, new errors can get slipped into the memory weakening parts or boosting others based on new experiences and information.

Thankfully this one type of bias can be eliminated rather easily if a scientist just does proper note taking and goes through the peer review requirements. That alone is enough to purge nearly all of these biases. It's why in GMP, the procedure for anything to go into the human body, the scientist has to record and document everything they do exactly at the time it was done or it no longer counts, as no one wants their health risked by the fallibility of human memory.

Part 2: Taoism After Lao-tzu

"A frog in a well cannot discuss the ocean, because he is limited by the size of his well. A summer insect cannot discuss ice, because it knows only its own season. A narrow-minded scholar cannot discuss the Tao, because he is constrained by his teachings. Now you have come out of your banks and seen the Great Ocean. You now know your own inferiority, so it is now possible to discuss great principles with you."
-Chuang-tzu

Chuang-tzu

Lao-tzu's supposed successor Zhuang Zhou, or Chuang Tzu allegedly wrote the second most important book to the Taoists, the Chuang-tzu, a much longer book written with wit, irreverence and spontaneousness, and is considered one of the most influential works of literature in Chinese history. It is a book made to force you to think beyond what you know. One example from the book is the Dream of the butterfly in which he dreams he is a butterfly and then when Chuang Tzu wakes up, he questions whether he was a man dreaming he was a butterfly or he is actually a butterfly currently dreaming he is a man.

Uncertainty is the center of his book because the second you become certain of anything, your mind stops questioning and you can easily get stuck in an untruth. It is because of this that it has been said that science is not completely certain of anything. It is, however, agnostic with degrees of certainty. The more data, and better the methods of weeding out statistical anomalies and personal bias that science develops, the more certain one can be. However, one can never be 100% certain of anything, which is why scientists so often use words like "might be," "possibly," "probably," and never "is." Even though the chances of them being wrong is microscopic on some topics, they still refuse to use terms that describe it with full certainty.

To the layperson, facts are hard and solid things. Quantified nuggets of never changing truth. While growing up, I collected facts. I unfortunately had no idea how many qualifiers these facts actually had and how often they only worked in certain situations. I really enjoyed chemistry, but I didn't realize that I was given a fake shell of an understanding to start me out.

It's all way more complex than what they teach you and takes years of learning to fully grasp. I treated every rule of first year high school chemistry like it was a solid certain fact. I would run stoichiometric calculations in hopes of figuring out how to make new chemical compounds. For those who don't know, stoichiometry is a way to

calculate the beginning and ending products of a chemical reaction. I would experiment with legally attainable chemicals and rarely get the results I wanted or expected and energy input, bond shape and catalyzation had yet to be taught to me.

I did the same thing with string theory. I took all the pop science facts I knew about string theory and used some brilliant and innovative thinking and created my own "theory" to explain it. Had all the facts been solid and correct and as simple as I thought they were, I may even then have not been right. I would have had to find a way to disprove it in the real world and I didn't have the first clue how or even why to do this. I hung on to the idea in the back of my mind until around 15 years later when I picked up a book by Brian Greene and discovered all of the "facts" I thought I knew about quantum physics were true but not solid, and there was an entire universe of what I was oblivious to in science and how and why we know what we know.

Easy is right

Chuang-tzu says

Eazy is right. Begin right and you are easy
Continue easy and you are right
The right way to go easy is to forget the right way and forget the easy going is easy.

It is said that easy in this case means natural. Your natural state according to the Taoists is also egoless. Being egoless, you will naturally be guided toward right and it will be easy for you to distinguish the two. What was the point of the struggle? Why is good treated as being so hard?

Because, Master Chuang says, the ego likes the difficult, it likes the challenge. Ambition is a challenge; piety is a challenge. But when the ego is taken out of the equation, according to Chuang-tzu, doing the right thing becomes natural and easy.

Master Chuang of course knew nothing about cognitive biases and how many of them are very natural and unwittingly lead you to wrong instead of right. Being egoless is essential to facing your biases, but that's not all you need. It still requires lots of work and effort to keep on top of things, however one's ego and identity can make even the smartest person believe the dumbest thing if it's based on their identity. One's identity means a lot of different things. Their religion, their political party, their ethnicity, their nationality. If someone attacks these strongly held beliefs, they are attacking one's identity and one can get very emotionally and irrationally defensive. It shuts down all communication. It makes the person dig in and rationalize their belief even deeper.

If a person has no tie to a belief or even a very weak tie to it, they can easily change it with new evidence. One must be ok with the discomfort of not knowing, and train oneself to overcome their need for

closure, which is incredibly natural and the easy route. Once you understand how your mind works it becomes easier, but even leaving your ego out of it the biases will plague you no matter what.

Turtle in the puddle

The emperor sent messengers to Master Chuang with a request that the Master become prime minister of his kingdom. Chuang-tzu was fishing at the time and simply pointed down into the water. "Do you see that turtle wagging his tail in the mud?"

"Yes," they replied with respect due.

"Do you see how happy he is?"

"Yes, Sir. He looks very happy," they replied, very confused.

"I have heard that there is a turtle in the king's palace, three thousand years old, dead, encaged and encrusted in gold and jewels. There he is worshiped. If you ask this happy turtle to switch places with the turtle in the palace, would that turtle be ready to accept that?"*

"No sir, this turtle would not be ready for that."

And Master Chuang finished, "Why should I be any more ready than this turtle? I am happy with my mud, wagging my tail and I don't want to come to the palace. Worshiped and encrusted with jewels, dead, trapped in a cage. Be gone!"

This story is interesting because it creates an ethical dilemma. He could have used the power to make great good for the people. But he would not be happy. He may have known just how much power would corrupt him. He may have believed that even

181

if he did good, the cycles and annals predicted that all of his accomplishments would cycle back to end up being meaningless. He may have known the king or lords would have limited him from doing the unpopular things needed to make a just system. Or he may have just selfishly wanted to stay happy, keeping out of politics and letting the world go on with injustice even though he had some power to stop it.

Death, violence, and abusive unelected leaders were normal. They always existed and never would go away. Paying attention to injustice is stressful and if you believe you can't change anything, you can keep your head down, be normal and live a life mostly stress free. Perhaps in our modern day with science, this idea should be rethought. Things can get better and the moral arc of the universe is bending ever more slowly toward justice but only if we take a stand.

This is an idea of the privileged, or those who are fatalistic and given up hope for something better. I would love to stick my head in the sand and just live my life oblivious to reality and injustice in the world but the only way for evil to triumph is for good people to do nothing. What was going through his mind or the mind of his writer would be interesting to know.

Useless is just as important as usefulness.

Hui Shi, of the School of Names told Master Chuang. "All of your teachings are centered on what has no use."

The master replied, "It is only when you appreciate what has no use that you can begin to talk about what has use. Man uses only a little space at any one time. If you were to remove the space he isn't using, how long would he be able to use the space he is using.

Hui Shi replied, "it would cease to serve any purpose."

"That is why we must understand things that are considered to have no use."

The useless is incredibly important in science. The useless is free but still useless. The space in the house can't be bought or sold but is there anyway. Play is useless but it's found to be essential to build a creative, healthy, and productive mind. To subsistence farmers who were relying on crops just to survive, education was useless compared to working hard to grow crops but once education became common, more were able to create farming techniques and implements, which allowed one to work less to produce more. In fact, invention and tinkering is useless. Most of what you are going to make will end up useless and often in the trash. But by making enough useless things, you can end up making something very useful.

Meditation is useless. You are doing literally nothing, not even thinking about problem solving. Yet because of it, you can recharge and have useful thoughts that are more healthy and productive. You could be

using that time to work but you will burn yourself out and make more mistakes. Enjoyment is useless. Happiness is useless. Yet it still makes life worth living. In the book Descartes Error by Antonio Damasio, a man had his brain damaged in the area that produced emotion making, him all logical and brilliant but because he had no emotion, he had not even the slightest bit of motivation to do anything with that logic.

In science, studying the useless is essential. The breeding habits of a rare moth may be useless now but in the future all of

Play may be considered useless but Frodhi sure enjoys it

183

that time and research may lead to a new discovery in medicine or even biomimicry and it will turn out that research was needed. Air was considered useless but when people began studying it, they realized they could make it useful. People believed that there was nothing in a vacuum, but it turns out a Higgs field is there, which gives everything mass.

In a parable, Chuang-tzu said that a man had a donkey and he was traveling on a pilgrimage to a holy place. He was very poor and very hungry, having spent his last coin. So, he sold his donkey to another traveler who was rich. By the next afternoon the sun was very hot, and the poor man rested in the shadow of the donkey.

The new owner was frustrated and said, "You sold this donkey to me, get away from him."

The old owner replied, "I have sold you the donkey but not the shadow."

Things taken for granted and useless can become useful under the right circumstances.

Silence is useless to most people while talking is useful. But for some, talking just to talk to is useless and getting to the meat of the topic is useful. From a psychologist's viewpoint, small talk generates connections that can be useful in terms of bonding. In

the world of science, nothing is useless. Everything in science is useful. It serves a purpose and is essential, it is purely a subjective value placed by our minds that makes things useless.

Respect is not useful to Chuang-tzu, but it is to the average person. Chuang-tzu spoke of a man with a hunchback. The Emperor had a war and forced all young men into the military. However, he was useless to the military. If you are useless, no one can control you. You can be left alone. You are free.

He said, "Be alert and don't be very useful, or people will exploit you."

A tree that is all knotty and scraggly is useless to a person looking for wood to build with and they will leave it alone. But for a person looking for firewood, that tree is very useful. Make sure you are only useful to the right people in ways that they need. As science progresses, what is useless exists less and less. In the modern era, in a forceful draft like that, that hunchback could still have use for his mental faculties thanks to modern technology. In the modern era all of his arguments are paradoxes and that may have been his point then, to be a foil to legalism and flip the script just to get people to think beyond the rigid structures society had placed on usefulness and ego.

In a village where Master Chuang was passing through, the entire village was laughing. Laughing at him. That is because the

teacher was riding backwards on his donkey talking to his disciples. This is in Feudal China where appearances were everything and doing the slightest silly-looking thing could damage your honor. This sort of thing was not done.

The disciples were very embarrassed and distracted because they were seen with this silly man who seemed to care nothing about honor.

Finally, one asked, "Why are you doing this? You are making a fool of yourself and, by proxy, us too. We are being ridiculed unnecessarily! People think we are idiots!"

Master Chuang replied, "There is something great implied in that. If I sit the way one would normally sit on a donkey, my back is facing you, and that is insulting you, and I don't want to insult anyone, not even you. If you walk in front of me you will have your back to me, and that is insulting to me and it's not good for disciples to be seen disrespecting their masters. You could walk backwards in front of me but that is dangerous, and I don't want you to come to harm. We could also stop but we must move forward. So, this is the solution I have found and I can still teach even when we are moving."

"Let the fools laugh. We are facing each other. I am being respectful of you and you are being respectful of me. And the donkey has no objections, so why should we care at all what others think?"

Useless does not mean meaningless. Depression is a lot of work without useful results. In fact, one of the things one always wants to do when depressed is to try and think their way out of a depressive episode. Depression is exhausting without accomplishing anything. One of the best ways to deal with depression, aside from getting psychological help, is to do the useless thing of not thinking. You get tired and aching when you are sick. Quite often the virus or bacteria isn't causing that, your own body is doing that to get you to rest and stop moving. Your brain turns the natural background aches you already have up to 11 and it forces you to lay down and stop moving. Your immune system then uses that energy you are no longer using to fight the infection.

The same is true with your brain during depression. The brain has natural mechanisms to get one out of depression. Some are more resilient, and some are less, which then require medication. The best way to stop a depressive episode is the same way you fight a sickness, conserve energy, and become useless. Your brain has a limited amount of glucose that can be brought into the brain and a limited amount of waste product that can leave the brain. When thinking and focusing on your depression, you won't get enough of that glucose to the right areas of your brain needed to fix the depression. It feels useless but it's the best way to deal with the problem.

Chuang-tzu idealizes the perfect man who is in no way impacted by either admiration or hatred. He is egoless. The true or perfect man uses the knowledge he does have to discover the knowledge he doesn't have but many times he must collect knowledge that appears useless and wait for a situation where it will become useful. Until then, it sits idle. The useless knowledge can often blend with other knowledge or create different points of view that even if the situation never arises, the knowledge still isn't useless if it allows you a different angle of looking at a problem and a different lens of seeing the world. The true, perfect, or primordial man had no regrets, made no show of power and, if he was lucky, did not worry about the future.

Part of his primordial man is true, but there are things about anthropology that Master Chuang could never have known. The hunter/gatherer man followed the weather, had little use for collecting things unless for a religious reason. The idea of planning ahead wasn't necessary until farming came into practice. They didn't really plan ahead because they had tribal lore that mostly told them what to do, how to follow the herds, when to migrate. They had more of a collective planning ahead than an individual one that came about through generations of trial and error. Their knowledge was encyclopedic as to what food was edible and in which season. However, ego and power

are drugs even the primordial man had, but the tribes had a way to counter the worst of these things via leveling mechanisms.

The Shaming of the Meat is an interesting story about the !Kung people of Southern Africa by the anthropologist Richard Borshay Lee(1969), who, for a holiday in a village he was visiting, wanted to give the tribe a great feast. He bought the biggest ox he could find for the feast. When he told the people, especially the women, they insulted the ox, saying it was scrawny, even though it was exactly the opposite. They called him stingy, making fun of him. At his wits end, he asked some of the people he was closest to why he was being mocked instead of being thanked as he would in "polite society." A few of them took pity on him and filled

him in about what was going on. In their hunter/gatherer society, they understand the danger of power and how addicting it is.

When you can afford to give lavish gifts to people, the power balance shifts, creating a power imbalance which boosts the ego of the giver. Power really does corrupt, it's a drug and in a society like that, they can never afford to let it go unchecked. Instead, they will mock and shame the gift so that the giver doesn't get a taste of that power and gain an ego. This is especially true in young developing men as testosterone is a double-edged sword that not only makes us stronger, but also, when boosted too much, can make us stupid and reckless, something that would have spelled disaster in a pre-agrarian world.

The economist John Coates teamed up with neurobiologists to test the blood of Wall Street traders(2012). When men made a good trade, especially one that was risky, the testosterone levels in their blood would spike. They would then make riskier and riskier trades, often until they lost it all for themselves or their firm. During the last recession, much of the blame could potentially be put on young men chasing this testosterone high and doing stupid things as they made up most of the traders at the time. Women and older men without the testosterone addiction made much more rational, less risky trades that in the long term paid off more, but were weak and puny in the short term.

Men of some tribes would often operate the same way. They would leave the women to do the hard, low-yield work such as food prep, which had a higher long-term payoff, while they would go on large animal hunting parties to get the high of a short-term project with a lower long-term payoff. They would take this supplemental protein back to the tribe to trade for status and often sex. An advantage of this trade-off was that it made the men patrol their borders, reducing the chance of being attacked by a rival tribe unawares(Diamond 1997).

Tar pit paleontologists had for decades been very confused as to why they find a disproportionate amount of male mammoth bones over female ones. The more recent findings showed that young males were just like humans and much more likely to take risks, good or bad, and end up dying in rather dumb ways (Pecnerova, 2017). The "I have a penis, therefore physics doesn't apply to me" mindset still plagues us today, but even more so now that we have 2 ton death machines we call vehicles..

Those risks helped men mix with other tribes, to prevent inbreeding, or learn new things when the older generation had always done things a certain way and had a much less plastic way of thinking. Often, they would fail, but with enough dumb risks, one in several dozen would discover something useful to the entire group from the risk

taking which kept the trait in our gene pool. In other words, the perfect true primal man wasn't the way that Chuang tzu presents him as in a vacuum, it was the tribe, the elders and the women that made him those things.

Man thinks he is the best, but when compared to the Tao, he is nothing. Everything is futile, everything relies on nothing. Greatness is for ego alone. A true sage delights in an early death and old age, either are delightful to him. They are new discoveries and there are so many paths one can take that every new surprise both successful or failing is fascinating to the sage and delights when others can learn from the model and experiment that is life.

A scientist must be this way. Not getting the data you wanted might be disappointing, but one can always find something interesting in even failed data if they can look at the useless data and patterns. Or the data can be used by other scientists who are interested in trying that method but try

something slightly different.

Sadly, while that is the hope, our current scientific papers and academic grants are set up for the people to find new things and only the successful experiments are written about and applauded, while failures do not make it to the public.. There is no Nobel prize for failure, there is little grant money or tenure for science professors who never see new discoveries that fit the hypothesis. And no one gets noticed for reproducing studies unless it's a huge breakthrough, which leads to the reproducibility crisis we discussed earlier.

If you want to gain things and have your ego stroked, you will go after finding positive results, never showing what can't be done and, for decades, no scientific journal could afford to publish failed experiments. Thankfully, online open access journals are slowly becoming more and more acceptable to publish the previously considered useless papers so others will never have to fail that

way again as well, or to show that a formerly positive study is unreproducible, and therefore wrong. It takes a scientist not looking for their own ego boost to do this thankless work, and many are trying to make it more mainstream for all to do.

Of course, Master Chuang also goes into many of the traditional Taoist messages of not interfering so much with nature and doing as little as you can. Being the most precise and least invasive. Going with the flow of nature, not against it. Horses eat grass, run around, and have manes. That is what a horse is for, but then a person comes along and claims that they are good with horses, trims them, whips them, brands them, races them, forces them to pull things or be ridden and ties them up. The same is true with the "Sage." Humans do what humans do naturally, then the "wise sage" comes along and hands out idealistic and unnatural rules and people now are compelled to follow these rules and are punished if they don't. This turns a natural human into an evil human when there was nothing wrong with the human to begin with.

A true ruler interferes the least and uses human nature to rule instead of imposing unnatural ideas. Going with the tide instead of against. It made humans discontented with what they had, aiming for an ideal that could not be reached because, like horses, they have a nature of what they are, and trying to reach an ideal generates a greed for wisdom and a fight for power and wealth.

People who try to lock up treasure in chests and well protected boxes appear wise but when a great thief comes along and just takes the chests and boxes, you just made it all the easier for him to steal it. Organizing, weighing, measuring, sorting, packaging, all makes it that much more convenient to the thief. Making rules and laws and morals, makes it all the easier for someone to come in and abuse and hack those rules and morals through manipulation and rules lawyering. With these rules, morals and laws, you can steal a nation, and no one can touch you.

Master Chuang-tzu literally says, "He who steals a belt buckle pays with his life; he who steals a state gets to be a feudal lord-and we all know that benevolence and righteousness are to be found at the gates of the feudal lords."

Thousands of years before the quote, "If you rob a bank, you get arrested. If you own a bank you rob everyone with no repercussions."

It's like nothing changes.

Chuang-tzu even goes so far as to insult the revered Yellow Emperor from the mythical Xia age, saying he used benevolence and righteousness to meddle with and bend the minds of men. And even then, he and his future rulers couldn't entirely bend people's will perfectly as many rebelled, requiring banishment, imprisonment, and death, because it goes against the nature of humans to be controlled and their minds meddled with.

He discusses how people only like being with people like them, and hate being with people who are different because they want to stand out from the crowd. They want to be a unique individual just like everybody else. Go with the crowd, be part of the mix of human differences instead of using your desire to make yourself unique, it makes you hate other people who are different.

The 8 immortals

Before we move on to the final Taoist book we will discuss, we have to talk about the Chinese view of life and death. Taoism focused very little on life after death. For many in a certain branch of Taoism, it was believed that once you died, you were just dead, your spirit however lived on it the dao, just like how Obi-wan and Yoda lived on in the Force. However, because they believed that hatred, pride and unnecessary violence did not exist in nature, it was unnatural and therefore wrong to look down on other religions. This of course was not often observed especially when Taoism had the favor of the ruler in charge, however because of this it was often in the political underdog position in China to Legalism or Confucianism.

Over time it ended up merging with neo-Confucianism and ancestor worship and other folk religions and became known as being synonymous with all Chinese folk religions. At the time, though, it was just a branch of the hundred schools and believed it was all over after death. It clashed politically for a bit with Buddhism when it came into China with reincarnation vs the end

at death, but over time they figured out a way to live peacefully with each other. The Immortals, however, are a radically different bunch of characters. Some high, some low, some beautiful, some ugly, showing that anyone could become immortal no matter their culturally assigned worth.

A branch of Taoism developed from that belief of no afterlife that using various methods one could gain immortality similar to the obsession with eternal life that Emperor Qin allegedly died of. Many believed there were various ways to attain immortality using nature and understanding the Tao. This immortality cult believed that one could achieve it using alchemy, long meditation and even ejaculation avoidance, believing semen to be a source of life as it created new life. Using certain pinch points one can stop an ejaculation, though what it does is cause it to backflow into the bladder and you just lose it later when you expel it.

A certain sect of Taoist Women on the other hand developed what was called the "Order of the White Tigress," and believed that using semen from a man and meditation, they could also receive immortality similar to a western succubus, though viewed in a positive light. As Taoist men were preventing theirs from leaving their body (even though it did) it was only natural that Taoist women had to go out and collect it from non-Taoist men, most often through prostitution. As sex was natural and exchange was natural, there was nothing bad about it as "natural" is "good" in Taoism.

The 8 immortals were stories of people whom Taoists believed in or idealized as paths to gain immortality and they gained immortality by cultivating themselves to be perfectly in tune with Taoist ideals. Most were men, only two were considered female and one of those was intersex. They lived on an island paradise called Mt Penglai that only they could get to because of "weak-water" and normal boats would sink if they tried to sail on it. They had to purge themselves of everything non-Tao, therefore purging themselves and their spirits of disease and giving a gift to the old man of the South Pole, the god of longevity. They were more often normal people who, like the biblical Job, went through great suffering but without complaint and still gave of themselves to the people selflessly and the gods rewarded them with immortality.

Zhongli Quang

Born in the Han dynasty, this man, who is believed to be based on a real historical figure, has a long list of auspicious happenings at his birth similar to the supernatural things said about the Buddha, including light engulfing the room as he was born and speaking 7 days later with a very elaborate claim about himself. As a general, he fought against the Tibetans. His army was defeated in battle and he was forced to flee into the mountains. In that time, he met an old man who brought him to a secret spiritual sanctuary where he was allowed to stay for as long as he wished. There he learned the immortal rituals and a deep knowledge of alchemy. After only three hard days of

Zhongli Quang

193

He Xiangu

teaching, he was told to leave and use his newfound powers to serve his people. After turning to go, he turned back and the man and his home were gone. Using his power of alchemy and his magical fan, he created silver and gold coins from stones and saved people from poverty and famine.

Two stories tell as to how he became immortal. In one, his continual use of immortal powers and his magical fan eventually caused his descent into the shimmering cloud of the immortals. In the second, he was meditating near a wall of his hermitage when, behind the wall appeared a jade vessel that took him as an immortal to the shimmering cloud.

Zhongli is depicted with his chest and belly bare and holding a fan made of feathers or horsehair. He is known for his pleasing disposition and is often drawn while drinking wine.

He Xiangu

He Xiangu is the only woman of the group. When she was 14 to 15, she had a dream where she was told to eat powdered mica, remain a virgin, and gradually reduce her food intake. She later ascended to heaven during the Tang dynasty to be an immortal. He Xiangu's lotus flower improves one's mental and physical health. She is depicted holding the lotus flower, and sometimes with the musical instrument known as sheng, or a fenghuang to accompany her. She may also carry a bamboo ladle or fly whisk.

Zhang Guolao

Zhang Guolao is also based on a historical figure living during the Tang dynasty. He was a hermit who deeply studied alchemy, necromancy and the occult in general. He claimed to be several hundred years old and had, in his past life, been the Grand Minister of the mythical Emperor Yao around 3000 years prior. You will note that this was long after Buddhism came to China and the idea of rebirth became more infused into the doctrine. He loved wine and experimented with wine making from various plants and herbs. Because of this it was believed that his wine he carried gave healing properties.

He was also the master of qigong, a Chinese equivalent of Yoga but also could be used as a tool to enhance martial arts, and he was believed to be able to go for days on nothing but a sip of wine. He is often depicted in qigong poses. He was known to be quite entertaining by turning invisible, grabbing birds out of the air, and wilting plants just by pointing at them.

In art he is depicted riding his white mule, often backwards as a nod to Master Chuang. After riding around 1000 li(1 li = 1/3rd

Zhang Guolao

a mile or ½ a Km) he would fold up his donkey and put it away in a box. When he wanted to use the donkey, he would pour water into its mouth, restoring it. He would do anything to avoid meeting with kings and emperors including dropping dead and immediately being consumed by worms and being found perfectly healthy later.

He is often depicted with his emblem, the fish drum, which is a tube-shaped bamboo drum with two iron rods or mallets, or a phoenix feather or a peach, representing immortality. He can also turn into a white bat which represents permanence. Since he

195

most well-known and considered the de facto leader. He was born in the Tang dynasty. He was a poet, scholar and a master of internal alchemy. He is often shown in scholar's robes, with a sword that dispels evil. Most of the immortals have a flaw of some kind, his being a mean drunk. He genuinely works to help people attain immortality. He had an auspicious birth and became something of a child prodigy but failed to pass the civil service exam twice. He became a county magistrate, but the politics drove him to ruin and he retired to the mountains. There he passed Zhongli Quan's ten tests and became immortal. He is believed to stay on earth and not ascend to heaven until he has taught everyone the Tao and they are able to ascend too.

Han Xiangzi

Han Xiangzi was the final of these immortals that may have been based on a real historical figure and was said to be a disciple of Lu Dongbin. He is depicted carrying the Dizi or flute. He may or may not be based on a descendent of a famous historic Confucian figure. It is said that his grandfather Han Yu opposed and tried to dissuade the Emperor from supporting Buddhism and left in disgrace. He later wrote 3 poems about his grandson that went down in history as great poems. A source shows that Han Xiangzi may have been an official at the Ministry of justice.

Lu Dongbin

represents old age, in the Feng Shui tradition, a picture or statue of him can be placed in the home or bedroom of an elderly person to help bring them a long life and a good, natural death. A picture of him on his mule offering a descendant to a newly wed couple can also be found in Taoist nuptial chapels.

Lu Dongbin

Of the immortals Lu Dongbin is the

In the stories, Han Yu, who acted as his adopted father after his brother died, tried to push his Nephew (in these stories, not grandnephew) to learn Confucianism and then later Buddhism to become a government official, but the boy showed no interest in either of those and preferred to work on perfecting himself in the Taoist way and remain a commoner. It's said he could change the colors on a flower with this knowledge.

You will notice depending on the time that in China, Buddhism was a way to political office of esteem, whereas in India it was meant to be the religion of the people and commoners who shunned power just as Taoists in China did.

Han Yu married Han Xiangzi to a wife but he never consummated the marriage or at least didn't have any children. Han Xiangzi ran off a few years later to join Lu Dongbin and Zhongli Quan to perfect his knowledge of Taoism. After he attained immortality he returned to Earth and tried to also give his uncle, aunt, and wife immortality but Han Yu was so obstinate in his Confucianism, it took magically showing up and saving Han Yu from a snowstorm to teach him about Taoism and the way to immortality. He was later able to do the same for his wife and aunt. Which would make that eleven immortals? Who knows? Myths and stories are all over the place.

Han Xiangzi

197

Lan Caihe

Lan Caihe

Lan Caihe was a traveling musician and performer who entertained the other immortals.

He was also born during the Tang Dynasty and has the appearance of a teenager of indeterminate sex. Some viewed him as intersex, some as a man who was supposed to be a women, meaning a trans woman in the texts. According to the Book "Immortal legend", they slept on ice during the winter and wore winter clothes in the summer. Lan walked with one boot on and made up strange and changing songs as s/he saw fit. Sometimes Lan appeared to be crazy, just making random sounds, but with their songs they made enough money to survive or give to the poor. Lan became a doctor at only 18 collecting medicinal herbs in the mountain to cure poor people and lived off the land with fruit and stream water. On their way to the mountains they found a sleeping man with a wound near his navel. Lan, being a doctor, sucked the wound of pus(gross) and put a paste ointment on the wound. The wound started to bleed and the old man woke up and told Lan to go fetch water in a basket to clean the wound. Lan did as told and failed because of course a basket had holes. The old man then told Lan to fill the holes with mud but now the water was muddy. Then, out of nowhere, a beautiful lady was standing by the old man and laughed,

198

suggesting to plug the holes with lotus leaves in a pool. This worked and Lan was able to clean the wound. The old man then told Lan to drink from a Lotus pool and suddenly Lan became lighter and could fly. The old man and woman were Zhong Liquan and He Xian'gu and they flew away together.

Cao Goujiu

Allegedly part of the royal family in the Song Dynasty. Cao opposed his younger brother who abused and bullied the subjects and engaged in corrupt practices. Cao in turn used his position to help the poor in hopes of making up for his brother's misdeeds. Cao's brother was then accused in the court for his misdeeds. Cao was so ashamed that he quit his career and lived in the countryside in solitude. During this time, he met the immortals Zhongli Quan and Lü

Cao Goujiu

Dongbin, who taught him Taoist magical arts. After many years of practice and cultivation, Cao himself also became an immortal. Cao is often depicted dressed in official robes and holding a jade tablet or castanets. He is also regarded as the patron deity of acting and theatre.

Li Tiegaui

Li was said to have been born in the Yuan dynasty around 1300AD, he was also supposed to have been a student of Lao tzu, which would have put him around 700BC assuming they aren't discussing an Immortal Lao and not one of the 8.

Li Tiegaui is probably the second most well-known and best loved of the

Li "Iron Crutch" Tiegaui

bunch, known as "Iron Crutch Li". While he was considered easily angered and ill-tempered, he was also kind to the poor, sick and elderly and would heal people with an elixir from his gourd. He appears to be an old ugly unkempt beggar, limping on his crutch with a gold band around his crazy hair, exemplifying the useless tree narrative and also gave people an incentive to help the poor and needy as it could secretly be old Iron Crutch .

Li started out in a cave practicing Taoism. Lao tzu first tried to tempt Li using a beautiful woman he had crafted out of wood. Li rejected and ignored the woman, and since he passed the test received a pill that made him never hungry or ill again. Lao then tempted Li with lots of money from bandits found on Li's land which a disguised Lao, as a passerby, tried to urge him to keep the money. Li said he had no interest in money and in exchange for this test, Li was given another pill to fly at great speeds.

Li is said to have been at first a handsome man, and had his spirit leave his body to visit the other immortals and told his apprentice Li Qing that if he was not back in 7 days to burn his body because it meant that he had ascended. At 6 and ½ days Li Qing found out his mother was sick and burned the body early. On the way to his mother he passed a dead beggar with a bad leg who he didn't have enough time to bury. As it turns out Li Tiegaui did return from heaven and

200

no longer had a body and had to inhabit the body of the recently deceased beggar who was grizzled, ugly, and lame.

Master Lao gave him his gourd, which he used to cure Li Qing's mother. Li Tiegaui could also live in his gourd as he changed size to fit it. Li Tiegaui was now the immortal associated with the poor, medicine and healing and was tasked by Lao to travel the world, healing the sick and standing up for the rights of the poor and weak. He was a trickster clown character often appearing to be weak, crazy and worthless then getting back at the corrupt and the powerful who hurt their subjects and abused their positions.

There are centuries of stories of myths and folklore around eight, most often to teach a message or moral. Now that we understand this immortality cult, let's go on to Lieh Tzu, who seems instead to counter that narrative and that we should instead embrace death and not even think about immortality, for that is not the way of the Tao.

Lieh tzu

Like many in Taoism. Lie-Yukou may or may not have existed. Some scholars actually translate his name to mean "a philosopher who never lived," indicating he was made up in the Chuang Tzu to act as an example of a great Taoist life. The book itself may have been a blatant forgery at some point, similar to how there are several gospels and epistles in the bible attributed wrongly to the apostles, including a third epistle of Timothy and an epistle of Barnabus. Second Timothy is also considered to be a forgery by many biblical scholars .

His book starts off discussing the multi-connectedness of the Tao. Man comes from germs or seed parts, grows from those parts, and everything is connected in the universe. Individuality is an illusion. We have no knowledge of what it's like to be dead. Death could be much better than life. Toil and struggle make up the world, perhaps death is our home and we are just visiting. Death is a new experience, so embrace it when it comes. It appears to be almost a counter to the immortality cult of the time centered around Taoism. Sort of a self-criticism of what Taoism had become.

Contentment and gratitude, being a man, being a person who lived is in and of itself an important part of Taoism. Richard Dawkins is known for saying, "We are all going to die, and we are the lucky ones as opposed to the countless multitudes that were never born." Leih-tzu said it thousands of years prior.

He also discusses that people are sad and grieve about dying and poverty, while he says most people are poor and we all die. Being poor is normal. so there is nothing to grieve about.

He discusses the circle of life, how when we die, we become other things as we

are broken down and integrated into other things. Since we are really all just one thing, there is no need to be sad about or fear death. Birth and death are illusions.

Unlike Chuang-tzu, he quotes the Yellow Emperor as an expert, discussing death, and how death is just returning home to his natural state. Fearing death is foolishness. Will heaven and earth die? I don't know, but worrying about that is like worrying that heaven will fall on you and the earth will fall away from beneath you.

A minister is asked if there is a way to truly possess the Tao. He laughed and says, "We only borrow the way. We can never possess it. Our bodies are just on loan to us by heaven and we will have to give them back at some point. We are stealing everything from the Earth and heaven, of their benefits. Food, light, hot cold, water and air. We take them from nature and use them to our benefit. This kind of theft is common and unpunished. It's when we end up stealing from humans that we are punished."

Master Lieh discusses his 9 years of training, going from thinking of things as good and evil to no longer putting a value judgment on things and back again. Cycling between the two every two years. Saying whatever comes to mind, then focusing on restraint. Because both are part of the way. The yin and the yang. One must accept and be good at both.

He mentions the value of not resisting, as a drunk is thrown from a cart, but because he is already limp, he is less likely to break something because he is more fluid than the one who is not drunk and resists.

He discusses Confucius also differently from the earlier Taoists, as a wise man who can spot a wise person, perhaps being purposely blasphemous to the rigidity of what Taoism of his time had become. There was a time later in China where neo-Confucianism blended with Taoism. There have been many iterations of Confucianism and Taoism, sometimes at odds with each other, sometimes harmonizing as they absorb new reasoning and knowledge and philosophy that their original creators never imagined, much like how we don't know how many ideas of Buddhism were original to Gautama Siddhartha, and how many came from his followers in the future and attributed the ideas to him.

Confucius sees a great swimmer and a cicada catcher. He asks them if they have a way (Tao). The swimmer says no, it's just natural, he just does what he's always done. Being born near the water, swimming is just second nature to him for his livelihood. So, his swimming is just instinct, just like how a person raised on land finds walking natural.

The Cicada catcher focuses only on cicada catching. When he tries to focus on other things, he can't catch many of them, but when he focuses only on one skill, he is like unto a god at that one thing.

This is akin to the confused idea of genius. People think a person who is a genius is good at all things. A genius is

someone who is really good at one thing, and many in their arrogance have spread pseudoscience because they are bad at other things and go beyond their own competence because they are told how smart they are. Dr Henry Heimlich invented the Heimlich maneuver and saved thousands of lives. People thanked him constantly for saving them and it went to his head and began going beyond his level of competence, trying to reach a new peak of greatness and hero worship and sadly spread really bad science and cancer "cures" that didn't actually do anything. He was really good at one thing and was a god at that one thing. This made him believe he was a god of all the things and he was just a gullible self-deluding sucker who gave bad advice and people who believed in his magical genius died from it. This can be hijacked by the powerful as the carbon industry has used people's blind reverence to genius and the Nobel prize to buy off some Nobel winners not in the field of Climate science to downplay or cast doubt on climate research.

Lieh tzu then takes these ideas farther, discussing that true 100% belief can make the impossible possible. It can make a person live forever, a person to walk through fire and accomplish great feats. It is the idea that you can't do something that makes that true as well. This idea of supreme faith exists in all religions. How much master Lieh believed in the idea or just used it as a metaphor, I don't know, but he discusses it a lot in his book.

He takes on the idea of greatness. Greatness means you are unable to not have people rush you and rely on you and want something from you. However, acting noble but not thinking of yourself as one can make you well loved, It is once you think you are noble that you cease to be great.

Next he discusses the paradox of dreams and what is real and what is dreamed. What happens in the mind, memory, and reality, just like Chuang-tzu's dream of the butterfly while also going to absurd mind-bending hypothetical stories. He discusses Mr. Yin of Chou, who abuses his servants, especially one who is old and weakening. Fellow servants question as to how he can put up with such abuse. He answers that when he dreams, he is king and lord, engaging in all kinds of pleasures, waited on by servants and concubines. It is so real to him. So, when he wakes up, this is just something he endures until he sleeps again. He is a king so what does he have to complain about?

Mr. Yin has the opposite problem. The more abusive he is and more pleasures he engages in while waking, the more of a slave he is in his dreams. His stresses of power and abuses toward people under him in his waking time piles on to his slavery in his dreams. When he asks a friend about this, the friend tells him that with all his power and having more than he needs, fortune is righting itself in his dreams. Mr. Yin takes it to heart and begins to treat his servants much better and his sleep improves.

This is a nice Scrooge story but in all reality, bullying others has been shown to reduce cortisol levels in people doing the bullying, also the richer you are, the more isolated you become from others and the more disconnected you get from normal people (Sapolsky, 1994). You become less trusting of anyone who may want to take advantage of your money. Being wealthy and powerful becomes normalized, and you are constantly competing with other people who are powerful and rich who are also isolated from normal people, causing more stress, causing more bullying. No one can tell you no, the law barely applies to you. The human mind has ways like bullying to offset the bizarre power imbalance one has when abnormally rich and powerful. It would be great if this kind of karma existed in dreams, but the stress and bullying often makes dreams in the abused worse and calms the dreams of the rich.

Confucius is asked about his 4 servants. He responds that one is kinder than him, one is more eloquent than him, one is braver than him, and one is more dignified than him. The person asking is confused and asks why they serve him instead of the other way around. Confucius responds that his kind servant can't control his kind impulses, and will do what feels kind even when he isn't actually improving the situation or making the other person feel the kindness meant toward him.

The eloquent man can't control his tongue and know when to shut up. The brave one has no caution and the dignified one is so proud he is unyielding. If they could control these extremes to be useful, he would bow to and serve them.

Lieh tzu also seems to like mocking his younger self and his own ignorance, such as when he believed himself superior to others in how he enjoys traveling, focusing on how everything changes, and everyone else just contemplates the sites. He was told by his master Hu-tzu that it appears that he is unaware of how he himself changes, while being self-deluded that he is superior for paying attention to how external things change. His journeys are pointless because he doesn't understand his own mind and how he himself changes. He stops traveling and focuses on meditation. But later his master esteems the greatness of travel but the best travel is wandering with no direction and contemplating everything equally.

His book is mostly a lot of epistemology questions using extreme ideas to make us question how we know what we know. Circling back to Socrates' idea, "I am the wisest because I know that I know nothing." Logical hypotheses could be wrong in the face of evidence, our experiences are very limited and our interpretations of reality could be wrong because our minds are imperfect. That is why in science, the best we can be is an expert at one thing with a very narrow field. and we understand the system and the methodology and how it works, and can attack someone's methodology, but beyond that, most of us are too ignorant to know if their conclusions are correct or incorrect unless they correlate with our field.

For this reason, scientists are more likely to trust science and its conclusions because we understand the methods and know the limits to our own understanding. Science is incredibly humbling, and it makes us all very aware of what we don't know if we are doing it right and have learned to reconcile with our own ignorance and be content with it, but always eagerly learning more. A person outside of science often doesn't understand the methodology, doesn't understand the null hypothesis. The person hasn't trained their mind to assume nothing and be conservative with what we can claim is true. They haven't learned to be content with uncertainty and still be eager to learn in the face of the never ending quest all while knowing that you always will be ignorant about the majority of the world.

Certainty is essential to people outside of science. This is why they are often so much more likely to distrust science and more susceptible to pseudoscience and conspiracy theory because they don't understand how and why we claim to know what we know. Science, to these people, is simply arrogant lies made for profit. We assume we know nothing beyond what can be proven.

207

As philosopher Karl Popper put it, "Science should never be used to prove anything, just to disprove claims as lacking evidence as one cannot disprove a negative". Once we have exhausted all of our attacks on a claim, we then accept it as reality for now but always utilize agnosticism with degrees of certainty.

It is a countering of a bias that our brains weren't naturally trained for and we must discipline our minds to get to the state where we understand science. Until we have that understanding, we won't begin to be able to understand science and even the barest hint of how reality works.

What did Taoism get wrong?

Well there are two problems with

Taoism, but the first one is mostly because early Taoism is so deeply steeped in what was just taken for granted in Ancient China and that is the belief in the Golden age syndrome of the Xia kingdoms. Though to be fair, Taoism was also a counter critique of Confucianism, Legalism and the School of Names, acting similar to Laveyan Satanism's relationship to Christianity and believing in the same mythos, just taking the opposite viewpoint. Lieh tzu and Chuang-tzu also appear at points to challenge this assumption, repairing some of the things just taken for granted as true by Lao tzu. Chuang-tzu makes even the venerated Yellow emperor look foolish and Lieh tzu makes the believed foolish Confucius look wise. This issue appears to be corrected through ambiguity by later Taoism.

As we can tell, other than pre-agrarian periods, life was in no way better the further back you go. We were malnourished under early agriculture, which made us less intelligent, less healthy and more violent. When we were hunter/gatherers, we lived around one person per square acre, though we often used infanticide or abortafactors as a method of population control to keep our numbers down. We were healthier as we lived a constantly on-the-move life, foraging year round in our territories. That doesn't mean violence didn't exist, it did, and we were rather distrustful of outsiders, but a bit more rational with a well-balanced diet.

When we switched to full on agrarian culture, we could feed 10 times the people per acre, but with a much less varied diet and archeologists can see the decline in health, bone strength and stature of inland agrarian cultures versus earlier hunter/gatherers. Rules were created not because we broke up reality but because we started living more densely together and they became required. But even while living in small tribes, we still had rules, ethics, and norms required by our ingroup.

The other flaw of Taoism is the idea that we are naturally good and will always do the right thing without rules. There is some truth to this, and we aren't naturally bad unlike what the Hobbsian and Legalist schools believed. The problem is that we evolved in a completely different setting and environment and we are living in a world we didn't evolve for. Oddly in some ways technology is actually making our environment more like

what we evolved for and in other ways it is forcing new environmental factors we as a species have never before experienced.

That said, even then we are still not naturally good. While it's natural to view the ingroup with empathy and altruism, like Mo-tzu discussed, it's abnormal to view the outgroup with the same level of empathy and altruism as our ingroup. We are also much more likely to blindly trust our ingroup over our outgroup.

When we can figure out how to work with the human nature as much as possible as opposed to against it, we will most likely have a much more peaceful world but until that point we will continue to struggle forward to figure out the best enforced rules

we actually need and discard ones we don't actually need that go against our nature. But we will still need mechanisms to make us aware of our own biases so that we know how to get around them via methodological skepticism, using the brain in ways it didn't evolve for just like we did with reading, writing, math and science. We have not reached even close to that point yet.

The Wisdom of the Asians and flawed Traditional Chinese practices

"The wisdom of the Asians" is a term used for a logical fallacy often falsely believed by people in the West.

Because the Chinese or Indians seem so smart, mystical, ancient, exotic, and mysterious, they must be right. I got sucked into my brand of pseudoscience often through this fallacy, where people would say, "this sold like crazy in Japan," as if that added to its medical legitimacy. Much of this idea was formed by noted mystic, theosopher and trickster Madame Blavtski who essentially created the myth that Marvel's Dr. Strange was based on where Asian Mystics had powers of astral projection, passing through walls, healing, hypnosis and levitating. These stories filled pop culture with the wise Yogi or Chinese mystic using Asian magical powers to win the day. The hippie movement ate this idea up whole hog and the new age movement carried the idea forward. We will be going over the list of things traditional mystical Taoism got wrong in terms of inventions that appear complex and beautiful but other than some meditative properties with possible placebo benefits, there is little to no science behind it.

The I Ching

During the Shang dynasty, forms of divination were created by throwing turtle shells on the fire and seeing how they cracked and split. As time progressed, more complex mathematical forms of divination were invented, one being the I Ching. This particular book involved three parallel lines either broken or unbroken depending on the trigram. One could toss a coin three times and find out what trigram you were

supposed to have. The math led to 64 different distinct trigrams each with their own meaning. From that you could potentially divine your future. Of course, just like with tarot, divination is pretty much useless as all studies have shown on randomness and bias.

However, both the I Ching and the Tarot aren't completely useless. When you engage in it by yourself, it gives you essentially a random prompt on what aspect of your life to self-reflect. When someone else reads it for you, it works like ancient psychological therapy, as the reader knows where to prod and what to ask based on prompts by the cards. Much of it is cold reading. Some involve knowing the person, or hot reading.

I have had my tarot read several times and while they were unable to predict anything about my future or know anything I didn't tell them, they did give out general good advice or allow me to focus on an aspect of my life in a light I hadn't thought of before, like a rough psychotherapist without any actual direction. As a mediation prompt or just fun, I Ching and other divination techniques such as casting the runes can be beneficial so long as you don't spend much money on it or take it seriously as a fortune telling device or believe that the random throw was a form of fate to tell you something.

The Chinese zodiac.

This is another form of divination, that takes your birth year, month, day, and hour and can give you specific random fortunes based on what year, month, day, and hour it is right now. Just like with the western zodiac, much of it is self-fulfilling prophecy, both internalized and from outside social pressure. Dragon year babies in China statistically do better than other years. However, more was expected of them and parents invested more time into their

Dragon children. Kids born in "unlucky" years had little expected from them, less investment, and less time spent on them because they were going to be nobodies anyway. And the data shows this out(Mocan & Yu, 2017).

The Chinese years are on a cycle of 60, with 12 animals each associated with one of the five elements. 2020 is the year of the metal rat, when Covid-19 broke out worldwide while the year Trump was elected was the year of the Fire Rooster and the Chinese people had a field day making fun of him with symbols of him as a cocky ridiculous rooster. Each symbol has particular traits just like in western astrology. The problem with any forms of astrology is they are all vague enough that what is called the Barnum effect takes over, finding patterns and significance where there are none. It's called that because PT Barnum noted that if you make something vague enough, people think it's about them. Modern Myers Briggs tests have the same effect, even though the people who created it had no background in psychology, they just hyped it, expanding on Freud and Jung's ideas.

Myers-Briggs has such an impact on workplace culture now that people have been passed over for promotions based on their results. Studies show that if you randomly assign grades and merit results to people, they begin to believe they deserve it(Ross, 1975). Even after they are told it was

100% random, it's hard for them to bring their egos back down or raise their self-esteem up. The people with the good scores think they are more awesome than they are and the people with bad scores think they are obviously not that great and got what they deserve. This is also why racism and sexism are so hard to overcome and studies show most often that men overestimate their own competency and intelligence, suffering from the Dunning Kruger effect, believing they know way more than they do on any subject, while women underestimate them-

selves and constantly suffer from imposter syndrome, thinking they don't belong and obviously people are going to find them out as inept even when they are smarter and more competent than anyone else around them(Cooper, 2018).

People are more likely to promote a confident person and if equally qualified people come in and one expresses more confidence than the other, the confident one has the advantage. Unfortunately, that has for decades given unfair advantages to abusive sociopaths or narcissists who are cocky and confident as all hell but self-absorbed and often abusive and manipulative, creating some terrible, unbearable workplace environments. When they reach the level of bosses, they often take credit for other's work(Ronson, 2011). Companies are just now beginning to attempt to control for that so they can get better, more empathic and nurturing leaders, even if they are less confident during the interview.

As a fun thing to follow or just like the I Ching, you use it for self-reflection and don't spend much money on it or just enjoy the aesthetics of it, it can be enjoyable. If you take it seriously as a form of divinization, the Chinese Zodiac just like the Western Zodiac can cause some harm.

Feng Shui

Expanding on the ideas of Yin and Yang, the I Ching, and the five elements, geomancy was developed to use math and geometry to divine where and how things should be built based on landscape, materials, colors, and space inside of those buildings. In some cases, they would observe the houses of successful people and see how they lived to find out what they had in common. They could afford an interior decorator for one and servants to keep the place spotless.

The Practitioners have maps of the 8 cardinal directions, each with an element

associated with it. Water Is north and cold, fire is south and hot. The other directions are figured out mathematically. Once again, just like with I Ching or astrology, in many cases you are given a number based on your birth year to tell you which of the eight cardinal directions are good luck and which ones are bad luck. You can place canceling or strengthening energy items, materials or colors on those places to adjust your luck. I used posters in college. Another example is if you happen to have your door at the money position you need to get a plant with leaves that are round and shaped like coins because otherwise it's a sign of your money draining away.

Avoiding sharp edges of tables and such pointing at areas where you often sit as it is believed to be psychologically disturbing.

Feng Shui has some good tips. Some are just good hygiene; others are good psychology. Some are good interior decorating and it will give you that Asian aesthetic, however, in several studies, no two Feng shui masters give even remotely the same advice, some telling a person to do the exact opposite of the other. If there was a real science to it, there would be a repeatable objective pattern. Instead, it goes more by gut feeling often and you just have to trust the person. In China, people take it so seriously, they will knock down an entire wing of their house to gain that good luck.

If it's all by feel, get yourself a pretty book on it, use it as a focusing point as a form of meditation, and go with your own conclusions. According to some "experts," you will have made the perfect choice and to others you will have just doomed yourself and your entire family.

Feng Shui is once again fun and it's great for meditation and aesthetics, but don't pay for more than a book and more than a fun hobby. Beyond that, you are flushing your money down the drain faster than not having a plant with money shaped leaves.

Traditional Chinese Medicine

Now this, like many subjects, has nuance. If you walk into an asian pharmacy or an acupuncture office you will be regaled with the thousands of years of ancient chinese wisdom passed down through masters that treat the cause not just the symptoms using the five elements and yin yang, treating the body holistically and such

Well that sounds great, but sadly it just ain't true. There was never a formalized system of traditional Chinese medicine until, oddly, the Chinese Communist Party took over. There were folk doctors and pharmacists, each with their own special combo of cures. Some that very much worked, some that were more placebo and belonging in the age of the humors when leeches were a normal thing.

The thing is, not only did

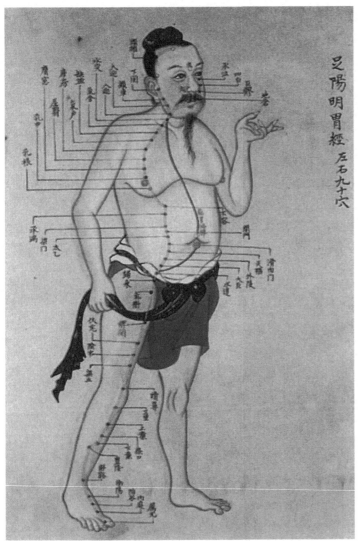

足陽明胃經

左右九十穴

Chairman Mao Zedong distrust doctors, possibly because of the distrust of their bourgeois mindsets, Mao also couldn't afford to send real medical doctors out into the rural regions. So, instead, he encouraged these folk doctors to ply their trade and promoted it as real medicine without the slightest evidence. This legitimized many treatments that may have been a placebo or done nothing, but that's what he banked on. When President Richard Nixon came to China, one of the odd curiosities he brought back was the idea of acupuncture. This and other elements of Chinese folk medicine fascinated the West and China began exporting it's "medicine" to the West, which required creating universities and a codified system out of jumbled together backwoods country doctors and the west ate it up (Levinovitz, 2013).

Acupuncture, when seen by Nixon, was used mostly to treat pain, which there is clear evidence for. Similar to how when you have an itch and scratch it to feel good because the scratch is interrupting the itch signal, acupuncture interrupts stronger pain signals. On top of that you have to learn to not move or the needles can hurt, forcing you to relax. Because you see real change, many believe you could treat all other ailments using internal energy pathways via the nerves that will stimulate healing and such. Cupping(using suction at specific points) and moxibustion(putting heat over the body at specific points), both give you the same impact based on the same energy pathways.

However, in blind studies, when it comes to pain reduction, a person off the street can literally put the needles in someone versus a master acupuncturist and still get the same result.

For any of the other things they claim it treats outside of pain, it fails in the face of a placebo. Oddly, toothpicks shoved into your skin actually caused more pain relief than the thin acupuncture needles.

From these studies, we have proven that

acupuncture is a great way to treat severe back pain. In fact people are using it to help them get off of opioid addictions they got on because they had unbearable chronic pain.

We are finding studies, especially in China, how one of their ancient herbs will show a chemical that treats a certain disease. Early healers most often didn't use herbs because they just convinced themselves of it. They saw a pattern of it doing something, even if it wasn't actually what they thought it was doing. However the methodology used in Traditional Chinese Medicine or

TCM and quite a lot of herbalism doesn't stand up to scrutiny. Inconveniently, unlike with synthetic drugs, every plant has different amounts of active chemicals just due to genetics or environmental variations, so it's difficult to do studies on herbs if the doses of the active ingredients are all over the place.

On a personal note, I was deeply into traditional Chinese medicine in my 20's. I was beginning to gain a gut instinct in understanding how to classify different things in different categories as prescribed in Chinese medicine, such as how

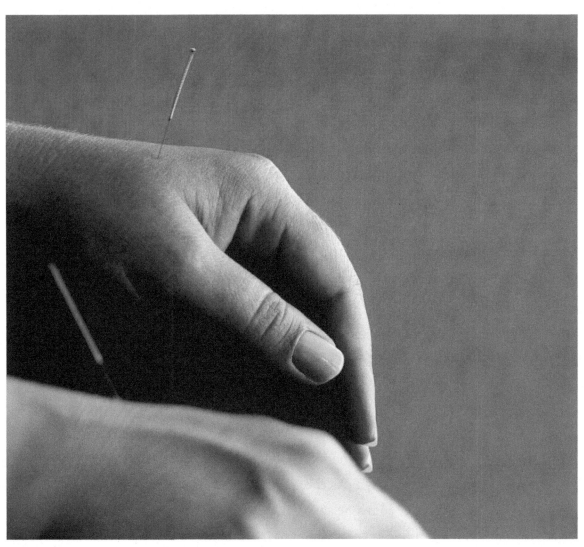

different food and herbs could have real – even if sometimes superficial – changes on the body. These could be found in the saliva, how hot you feel, and other small changes.

An example of this is when you eat spicy food with capsaicin and you feel cooler because your capillaries will relax or dilate more. Personally, I always had dry mouth and found Yarrow helped to treat dry mouth, an "earth element" herb.

Sadly, as with many things, if you see a surprising change, both you and the practitioner that is prescribing it can be convinced that it does even more than what it is actually accomplishing. Things like acupuncture, chiropractic, and even reiki become more than they were intended. Reiki which is from all studies essentially a parlor trick where someone focuses on making their hands hotter using biofeedback techniques that can have the same impact as a hot stone massage. Sadly, people can waste thousands of dollars on quack cures because they can feel a difference in their bodies, but they don't actually do anything for the problem at hand. If the person and the healer truly believe in what they are doing, they all believe they are doing good work.

Still, these cures can help as a placebo effect by creating a feeling of proactiveness, reducing stress and anxiety, sometimes even if you consciously know it is a placebo. Just the effect of going to see someone and spending time with a perceived expert who actually has and takes the time to listen can have a profound placebo impact. Feeling cared about and as if your problem matters is unfortunately often a foreign concept in the American healthcare system with overworked doctors suffering burnout, which may make Americans much more susceptible to this kind of "alternative medicine". Just having that human connection can have a big impact on your mental and physical health.

If that was all that there was to it, most alternative medicines would just be an expensive way to thwart stress. However, people will put their faith in these alternative cures and end up dying from easily treatable diseases because they didn't trust modern evil, "Western" medicine that has been peer reviewed and clinically tried repeatedly to the point that we know it has a much higher chance of helping with the problem. Asian nations produce and use cutting edge "Western Medicine" all the time. Treating folk cures as associated with one group of people is a form of noble savage myth. The west had an equal number of folk remedies just as beneficial and harmful for much of its history until modern chemistry and science was invented. Poverty, not benefit, kept these old medicines alive, and they had much shorter lives until science based medicine became available to all.

Also, aside from the herbs used, TCM and the Indian equivalent Ayurveda

will often also use minerals which probably acted as mineral supplements, though in some cases involved mercury, which while being something of an antibiotic back when they didn't have anything better, is still a poison. One interesting case was the use of dragon bones, which were actually dinosaur bones, leading most scholars to believe finding these fossils may have led to dragon myths being universal.

And lastly, we get to the use of exotic animal parts. When it comes to eating meat, certain animals are supposed to have different elements they are associated with, including dog meat. However, where things get dangerous is the use of animal parts, especially ones that are touted as being aphrodisiacs. Tiger and rhino parts being the most ecologically devastating and as the government cracked down on poaching to save their animals, the prices just kept getting higher and in places in both China and Southeast Asia it was considered a sign of manners and great respect to give people rhino horn. Sadly the western Black rhino was declared extinct because of this demand.

Shark fins for Chinese Medicine

When it comes to dealing with endangered species though, 2 factors are changing the norms and pushing down demand. First is a great education campaign that is slowly changing the minds of the people to move them to reduce or end this cultural practice as a way to protect nature and secondly is newer medical aphrodisiacs. People always make the joke that we can solve erectile dysfunction but not cancer. While funny, Viagra was a side effect drug from a heart disease study, and while it failed to treat heart disease, it ended up being able to be used relatively safely to treat ED. Laugh all you want, but many endangered species have more protection every year as people use Viagra over rhino horn and it actually works. Of course, because it was only tested on men like most studies, over time there is evidence that it can also treat menstrual pain, but as the patent is expiring, no one wants to spend the money on a clinical trial for it(Wiles, 2019). Another serious limitation of modern science that must be fixed as we move forward into the future, medical chauvinism. TCM has some medical secrets that need serious study and the Chinese government is investing a lot of money into the research, thankfully.

That said, the medical science at

this point shows few benefits for most of the herbs compared to more refined drugs. There is a belief that all of nature has a natural balance, so taking substances in herbal form has chemicals that can lessen the side effects. This is untrue; there are a lot of extra chemicals that we don't know what they do so we can't properly tell if something is useful or not. A plant only cares about one thing, making itself survive and reproduce. It really doesn't care about you, which is why there are so many poisons in the natural world. It's a war out there. Plants are literally fighting other plants or insects.

Some plants of the same species do work together, some of different species work together, but some are parasitic or invasive and just destroy the other plants using toxins only they can use. There is no magic balance in herbalism. That said, if approved by the FDA, most herbal supplements will not cause short term side effects. But we have no idea of the long-term effect. My mother would have me take pills of echinacea growing up because studies showed it increased white blood cell count, which, in layman's thinking, means stronger immune system.

That's not what that means in real life and long term studies showed that over time the white blood cells were abnormal and useless at fighting infection and the viable cells were actually lower if used for a long period of time (Kemp & Franco, 2002).

This is wishful magical thinking, the same thing that caused the great leap

forward fiasco in China and the Ukrainian famine, the first killing around 50 million and the second killing around 8 Million. Wishful thinking can work as a placebo effect but when things come down to great expense or life and death, death or scams are usually the outcome.

So there you have it. Traditional Chinese medicine touted as being ancient and handed down by the wisest of people like a sacred secret martial art was taken from a mix of old writings and backwoods "doctors" and turned into its own beautifully complex but unprovable field of pseudo-science. This was created to harken back to the ancient times, the same party that caused the cultural revolution and burned ancient texts and destroyed ancient artifacts to maintain Mao's cult of personality after causing the devastating failure of the great leap forward. Once again, TCM is not utterly useless. But just like with meditation, there are some really good benefits that require science, but that is the tip of the iceberg of the practice with the rest being neutral or harmful.

Part 3: Where do we go from here?

Both Buddhism and Taoism got a lot of things right and a few things wrong. I can say what I reject about them because, like all early theorists, everyone got it pretty wrong, but all got a little right, and there were around 32 different disciples from the Buddha who started their own schools and spread from him each with their own spin on it. There are around potentially 100 different writers of the Tao Te Ching and many schools from that. Each practicing in their own way. Each stuck on some form of dogma to the point of becoming unrecognizable to the others and missing the point of this all wise secular Buddha or Lao tzu figure, who almost certainly didn't say all the things they are attributed to say.

Some took ideas that were new at the time to an extreme, and some involved extrapolating on a mythical past they believed existed which had no basis in reality. However the strength of both of these philosophies, if not too dogmatically married to the religious part that helped spawn or preserve it, is that they have the ability to go where the new evidence takes them and take nothing on faith. In fact, doubt is a major part of their philosophies, just like science.

However both of these philosophies were created under the belief that there was an inevitable cycle to things and there was no real way to improve the world. It was actually the protestants that began changing this idea, and believed through science and self-betterment, they could make the world a better place. While both could have elements in their writings to deal with this paradigm shift, there is nothing explicitly said. There is a third more modern philosophy that deals directly with this idea of improvement through science that could help fill that gap.

Secular Humanism

Buddhism and Taoism have had their limitations discussed, however there is an applied philosophy that can fill in the rest of the gaps or synchronize the two and that is Secular Humanism. A philosophy with a relatively new history around the time that science made its greatest strides.

Secularism was first coined in 1851 by George Holyoake meaning "a form of opinion which concerns itself only with questions, the issues of which can be tested by the experience of this life." This sounds a lot like both Buddhism and Taoism. It didn't necessarily mean rejecting religion but it did mean that when it came to day to day experiences and how to behave and deciding the best methods for change socially and politically that one should use the scientific method and reason instead of using an appeal to the untestable supernatural.

Holyoake was also influenced by the Church of Humanity, a positivist idea by Auguste Comte, the founder of modern sociology, that human progress would go through 3 stages. These were the religious, the metaphysical or spiritualist, and finally a rational positivist society. He was also heavily influenced by the 1794 Cult of Reason, a state sponsored atheistic religion in revolutionary France to replace the Catholic church. It was heavy on fun imagery of reason, liberty, nature and the symbols of the new victorious revolution. They converted seized Catholic churches into temples of reason, and

226

held a festival of reason on November 10th where on the altar of reason would burn a flame symbolizing truth, while women and girls in white roman dress wearing tri-color sashes would mill about the room attending on the goddess of reason, who was liberty personified. Some dressed provocatively and often wore the red phrygian cap, a cap given to freed slaves in ancient Rome and most famous nowadays known to be the kind of hat the Smurfs wear. Lady Columbia, the precursor to Lady Liberty, was also often depicted wearing one of these hats. Living women were used to avoid use of statuary and idolatry. "To Philosophy," was written over the doors of the church. Of course, this offended enough religious Catholic French that the elected government was forced to return the churches their property after the reign of terror.

The Leicher Secular Society was first founded in 1851. Other regional societies formed to create the National Secular Society in 1866. Humanism started out as a religious concept by the ethical movement founded in 1793 in London at the South Place Ethical Society, now called the Conway Hall Ethical Society. The Ethical Society, created by Unitarians (who had not yet merged with the universalists) under the leadership of Reverend William Johnson Fox, much like the Quakers, supported female equality, giving a voice to Anna Wheeler, one of the first women's rights leaders in Britain.

Felix Alder brought this idea to the Americas and founded the New York Society for Ethical Culture in 1877, and over the next decade, more cities in the US had chapters.

These societies all adopted the same statement of principles:
- The belief that morality is independent of theology
- The affirmation that new moral problems have arisen in modern industrial society which have not been adequately dealt with by the world's religions
- The duty to engage in philanthropy in the advancement of morality
- The belief that self-reform should go in lock step with social reform
- The establishment of republican rather than monarchical governance of ethical societies
- The agreement that educating the young is the most important aim

Alder also believed that the belief that religion was required for morality led to religious bigotry, as the religious sects at the time, even in America, heavily distrusted each other, preventing true morality from deciding important social change. Therefore, the American branches adopted a completely neutral stance on religion, neither atheist, agnostic, or religious but a place for all religions or non-religions. British branches adopted a similar stance and the British branches joined together to form the Union

227

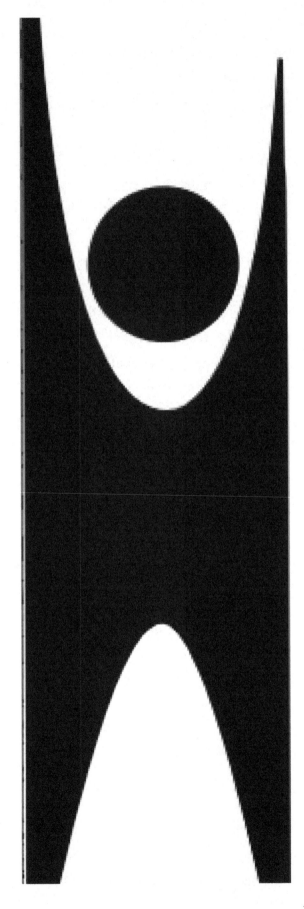

of Ethical Societies in 1896.

The first time the two were combined were in twentieth century sermons by Anglican priests, warning that "secular humanism" was destroying religion and Christian tradition. In the 1960's and 70's, certain groups began adopting this name as a form of humor and mockery. In 1980 "A Secular Humanist Declaration" by the newly formed Council for Democratic and Secular Humanism (CODESH, later the Council for Secular Humanism, which with CSICOP in 1991 jointly formed the Center for Inquiry and in 2015 both ceased separate operations, becoming CFI programs) gave secular humanism an organizational identity within the United States.

Other groups such as Humanists International and American Humanist Association believed that adding secularism had too much baggage due to vilification by religions and made it appear sterile and not focusing enough on the humanity part of it. Because of that, they never include secular or any other adjectives onto the name and treat it as uniform across all people even though secular in most nations means not exclusive or giving special treatment to religion or lack thereof.

Various Humanist manifestos have been created, each newer one adding onto the last as new ideas of ethics evolve and gaps are found in the current manifesto.

The original signers of the first

Humanist Manifesto of 1933 declared themselves to be religious humanists. Because, in their view, traditional religions were failing to meet the needs of their day, the signers of 1933 declared it a necessity to establish a religion that was a dynamic force to meet the needs of the day. However, this "religion" did not profess a belief in any god.

According to the Council for Secular Humanism within the United States, the term "secular humanism" describes a world view with the following elements and principles:

The need to test beliefs – A conviction that dogmas, ideologies and traditions, whether religious, political or social, must be weighed and tested by each individual and not simply accepted by faith

Reason, evidence, scientific method – A commitment to the use of critical reason, factual evidence and scientific method of inquiry in seeking solutions to human problems and answers to important human questions

Fulfillment, growth, creativity – A primary concern with fulfillment, growth and creativity for both the individual and humankind in general

Search for truth – A constant search for objective truth, with the understanding that new knowledge and experience constantly alter our imperfect perception of it

This life – A concern for this life (as opposed to an afterlife) and a commitment to making it meaningful through better understanding of ourselves, our history, our intellectual and artistic achievements, and the outlooks of those who differ from us

Ethics – A search for viable individual, social and political principles of ethical conduct, judging them on their ability to enhance human well-being and individual responsibility

Justice and fairness – an interest in securing justice and fairness in society and in eliminating discrimination and intolerance

Building a better world – A conviction that with reason, an open exchange of ideas, good will, and tolerance, progress can be made in building a better world for ourselves and our children

The humanist manifesto III was signed in 2003, including 21 Nobel Laureates.

The newest manifesto is deliberately much shorter, listing six primary themes, which echo those from its predecessors:

-Knowledge of the world is derived by observation, experimentation, and rational analysis, or empiricism.

-Humans are an integral part of nature, the result of evolutionary change, an unguided process.

-Ethical values are derived from human need and interest as tested by experience. (See ethical naturalism.)

-Life's fulfillment emerges from individual participation in the service of humane ideals.

-Humans are social by nature and find meaning in relationships.

-Working to benefit society maximizes individual happiness.

Other than a few minor areas, humanism, secular or otherwise is a positive addition to Buddhism and Taoism, rounding out what they may be lacking just due to their lack of information and understanding of science at the time. Now this trifecta is probably what I would consider the most complete and beneficial applied philosophy based on the science we have. That said, it may not hold up as much in the future and may require some additional ideas tagged onto it that technology at the moment doesn't exactly require.

Yugen

Many people say they are spiritual but not religious, which is an extremely ambiguous word. The word spiritual in the West is pretty much owned by the supernatural. That warm fuzzy feeling of the greatness and vastness of a higher conscious entity or entities out there.

This feeling is that emotion we get when we stare into fire, when it's believed our ancestors had a mental piece of mind for the first time, to question and think about reality around them as the fire kept their predators at bay. From there, like children today, we began to question how everything around us worked. This emotion from fire may be very well the reason the Indo-Aryans revered fire so much, which later evolved into the Zoroastrian religion where fire is one of the most holy symbols,

Of course, children are shown to look for agency in everything for better bonding, so it made sense that there were forces in the universe that were controlled by intelligent forces. Animism and spirits explained things that couldn't be otherwise at the time, and when they looked at nature, they felt an emotion often referred to as spiritual with the belief in the supernatural. As time went on, networks increased, agriculture allowed for cities and the kingdoms, and as kings became more powerful, so did the spirits, and they became in charge over more and more things, until there became one great spirit in charge of everything.

Great temples and cathedrals were built to help invoke and maintain the feelings of spirituality as the experts in the spirits were limited in information and knowledge. But from those networks, another force was rising from this view of the world. People began to ask questions of everything, what things were made of, how and why we loved, even questioning the existence of the spirits. They developed reason, debate, and logic. They began to develop many, many logical explanations for everything. They purely used arguments to try and figure out who was right about the world and the best one at arguing won.

Sadly, this way of viewing reality not only did not create spirituality for the common person, it was pretty much a toy for the rich. Just like how great technology including clockwork to steam power was kept as trade secrets from everyone and only available to the rich as novelties. Learning was a luxury for the rich. At a certain point trade began ramping up and philosophers began realizing that two completely logical arguments could be at odds, so they decided to go back to another of children's traits, experimentation. They decided that they could base their logical hypothesis on evidence.

This advanced our knowledge incredibly, though still in the realm of the wealthy, but in 1802, Johann Beckmann, an economics professor in Gottingen University in Germany called for opening up the useful arts and teaching many in a "systematic order" of the art. He created the very first curriculum in the teaching of Technology. With this shared knowledge of technology, this new method of discovering reality exploded, moving faster than ever in history and each new discovery built on the next new discovery. Psychology opened up our minds and allowed us to see that much of what had kept us from discovering reality was our own biases, of which there were multiple that were wired into us from evolution, and people like Richard Feynman pushed hard to make science incorporate them into their methodology.

Science was now a force used by both good and evil and spiritualists and fraudsters felt threatened. They began banding together politically and through propaganda to discredit science, as it did not do anything for you spiritually, so don't believe it or learn it. Carl Sagan helped define rules for skepticism to allow you the best communication and ability to prevent fooling yourself with your own biases and helped start a movement to counter that anti-science movement.

Science is amazing because it has evolved and continues to get more and more precise like a lens showing more clarity with each new grinding. It allows us confidence without belief, astronomy, where we used to look at the stars, we now can detect planets around barely non- visible specks in the sky. Mathematics went from a branch of philosophy, and many times religion in numerology, to a field of computing that created machines that can calculate with accuracy way beyond anything imaginable. The natural sciences advanced from cataloging the world's odd diversity with no explanation as to the why, to creating the best understood unifying theory in science, natural selection to the point where we can even analyze our own blueprint and make repairs and changes.

Many people call themselves spiritual and not religious. They believe that science is cold and sterile, and is just there to ruin the magic and mystery of the universe. The process of science is sterile and many times boring. But the outcomes that we can have with certainty and what we can accomplish fill me with wonder and excitement.

In China and Japan there is an entire school of philosophy on aesthetics. This school

involves the concepts of wabi sabi, or mindful beauty in the temporary, incomplete and imperfect. The art of kintsugi is one you will

find where if a bowl is broken, the beauty of the breakpoints is preserved by gluing the bowl back together using gold or silver. Organic and imperfection are beautiful.

Another idea is that of yugen, an idea that means different things in different contexts. In China it means deep, dim, and mysterious. In some Japanese writings it refers to subtle profoundness, many times in things that appear mundane. As it is part of aesthetics, it is referring to an emotional feeling of beauty or "An awareness of the universe that triggers emotional responses too deep and mysterious for words."

Japanese Author Kamo no Chomei describes it as "*When looking at autumn mountains through mist, the view may be indistinct yet have great depth. Although few autumn leaves may be visible through the mist, the view is alluring. The limitless vista created in imagination far surpasses anything one can see more clearly*" (Hume, 253–54).

To move forward with a science and humanist based world, we must first spread this idea of Yugen so that the average person can experience our thirst for beauty through reality, reason and science even if the process itself is boring and many times sterile. We must convince them to find that the known

that destroys old magical thinking to be just as profound, beautiful and emotional, or we won't be able to convince them to come along with us to a brighter future of what can be.

I feel connected to the universe in my understanding, in ways ignorance and naivety never could for the sake of mysterious magical feelings. With each new discovery occurring daily, my excitement grows as it opens up new questions and mysteries. I don't need to stay ignorant to get the feeling of mystery. The more I know, the more mysterious and artistic the universe becomes. That is why I am not religious; I am not spiritual. I have discarded the supernatural and embraced the core idea but with more understanding, the emotion of yugen.

"To watch the sun sink behind a flower-clad hill. To wander in a huge forest without thought of return. To stand upon the shore and gaze after a boat that disappears behind distant islands. To contemplate the flight of wild geese seen and lost among the clouds…"
~Zeami Motokiyo

Transhumanism

Transhumanism is an idea created by the realization that humanity will almost certainly reach a pinnacle of technology where we will begin to alter the human mind and body. While we have always idealized and had stories of humans with enhanced powers and abilities, until now we haven't been able to even consider some of the amazing enhancements the human body could have in the future. Thanks to advances in gene editing, along with new concepts like 3D organ and tissue printing, it could be possible over the next century to continue to exponentially increase one's lifespan to the point of near if not full immortality.

The singularity is a point in computer evolution where the physical size of a circuit matches that of a human brain with the same amount of processing power. If things continue to miniaturize as they have been, following Moore's law, where processing power doubles for the same space and price every 1.5 years, this will be reached between 2045 to 2050. There are current doubts as to if Moore's law will continue to hold up as we hit new limits to the physical size and atomic

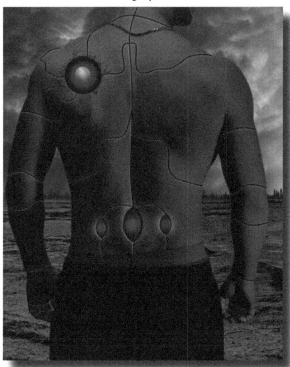

barriers, but so far we have squeezed out some new additional technology just in time to keep up with Moore's law. That said, once we reach Singularity, adding to or replacing damaged parts of the brain with better features may end up becoming the norm.

All neurological damage may be reversible, and psychological treatment may become much easier with new drugs and processing power to help the mind change. At the moment human brains are the best pattern seekers while computers are best at mathematics. Human brains are a jack of all trades master of none, while deep learning becomes a god genius of one specific task and bad at everything else. However, that may change. IBM has made a unit that mimics the inputs and outputs of a single neuron, though it is currently the size of a small computer, and we have 86 Billion neurons in our brains alone. Once perfected, scaling this down may make computers just as good at pattern seeking and versatile as humans. There is also the issue of quantum computing, which is currently in its fetal phase, that will add even more capabilities to our possible mental power in the future, especially our blind spot when it comes to stats and probability.

In the future we could all be extra smart, have our biases greatly reduced and have the ability to be warned when we are potentially falling prey to a bias. Our body parts could be just as replaceable as that of

any machine grown and made out of one's own stem cells. We may even create newer organs no one has thought of before, such as a super spleen for killing cancer cells and boosting stem cells in the blood for easier repairs and combat aging. Nanobots may go through the body doing cellular level repairs or purging heavy metals and toxins from the body. We could even repair our germ/ stem cells on a genetic level, picking out

genes that make us susceptible to cancer, and adding new genes that make us bigger, faster, stronger and smarter.

For a transhumanist, attempting to actively push us to this point is a moral obligation. They also have to tackle the inequalities of who gets this technology and who does not, meaning our entire political and economic systems may require an overhaul. Otherwise there will be a ruling class of ubermensch with massive advantages that the rest don't have and an impoverished dystopian subclass with even less power than our current income inequality allows for.

The ultimate idea is that of uploading one's mind to the cloud as a backup if one were to die. This could also be used for space exploration where the mind is shot out into the universe via a signal, to be picked up in the future by a robotic body that is indistinguishable to the owner to that of a human body, to explore and live on some planet. The human/robot on that planet will daily send their experiences back to Earth to be experienced by the person on Earth. Of course, this could be light years away, so tackling the mental discomfort of having the mindset of the you from 10 years ago shoved back into your current head could be a difficult issue to overcome. This is of course assuming you can put memories into a meat brain the way you can a computer.

Frankly though, I would not classify myself as a transhumanist. I see it less as something we should strive toward and more a natural advancement in science. Much like how plastic surgery was developed to help disfigured people and now is also used as an elective surgery to make people look more the "ideal human," all of these technologies will start out helping people with current diseases and disabilities and it will then trickle down to the able-bodied population. The question then becomes "is it ethical and an ideal to strive for?" That I do not know yet. Why? Because we don't know all the impacts it will have on humanity and each new advancement will need to be weighed and judged based on these advancements. To say one is for any future technology is like saying one is for nuclear power in the 1920's before we knew the destructive power and side effects it could have.

I am glad there are parts of transhumanism working to ensure the ethics of privacy, invasiveness and humanity, but those are and will be in the future just modern ethics and humanism. I view what transhumanism strives for as just an inevitable future, but only if we can continue with science at the rate we are currently at, and even sooner if accelerated. There is the argument that without death, our humanity will be gone, and our mortality drives us to do greater things. That is only really true if you aren't suffering from crippling depression or mental illness, and many would love to live long enough to get to enjoy this thing we

call like living after we develop treatments to help drastically with mental wellness.

There are also the ethical or moral arguments that trying to play god is blasphemy and hubris or just plain evil, but we've been playing god since we first invented glasses, extending the eyesight of people by decades, and our medical and agricultural advances have doubled our lifespan over a century. It's happening and we are doing it right now slowly, and people are fine with what would have been considered playing god and blasphemy by the church a hundred years ago.

The issue then comes down to not if and should we create immortality but how to fix the potentially broken applied philosophies we have once death is ridiculously rare or even potentially impossible without one's choice.

Immortalism

When you tell people about the idea of life extension, or living forever, many people who haven't given it much thought will balk at the idea, saying, "I don't want to live that long." Or, "Why would I want to live longer when life sucks so much?" Or "We shouldn't play god." Or "Death is what motivates me. If I knew I had forever, I wouldn't be so driven now." All these mindsets are pretty well set by older and modern philosophy and religion.

To be honest, the world as we have

Charles Napier Kennedy (British, 1852–1898), 'The Fountain of Youth', 1892

mortal was better because, well, it made us feel good about ourselves since we couldn't change the fact that we were going to die. In our lifetime, that could no longer be the case if we invest in science at a rate that we should and could.

Over the past decade, I've had these same anti-tech discussions with people about autonomous vehicles. People don't trust them, they like driving, they fear it will reduce their choices. Perhaps less people will drive but then perhaps less people need to drive. Perhaps it will increase insurance costs. Humans are actually pretty bad drivers and have horrible reaction times. 30-40k people die yearly from car accidents in the US alone. This was going down with the successful crackdowns on drunk driving, but then went up with texting. We are terrible drivers. All that would have to happen to make a robot drive better than a human would be to reduce its fatality rate by 5%. So far, almost all fatalities and accidents from autonomous vehicles have been operator error, not the fault of the AI. But people prefer the devil they know to the devil they don't and distrust anything they aren't used to. Fatalities from autonomous vehicles may have to be down to less than 1% of current driver fatalities for people to trust autonomous vehicles.

However, just imagine if we didn't have to spend so much time driving. You could sleep or get ready for work on your

it now is pretty messed up. It has always been messed up. That said, we know it could be something better. For some they have a fatalistic view of death. They view their life as finite. In theory, that may not have to be the case in the future. Until now, it was all just hypothetical, just as reasonable to hypothesize about as teleportation. It made for a great Star Trek episode, or twilight zone, and often came to the conclusion that being way to work. You could focus on other things such as reading or TV. I for one enjoyed the DC metro when I took it on weekends because I felt more at ease and didn't have to focus on anything. Also, automated cars could communicate with each other, reducing traffic jams and getting us all there faster. People who are disabled and unable to drive would now have increased mobility they never had before. Elderly would be able to get around. One's options would skyrocket. Being forced to drive everywhere eats away at so much of your day, especially if traffic is heavy caused by accident prone drivers who all think they are above average.

Just one person slowing down at the right point in traffic can cause a domino effect that can cause a jam up. There are many good reasons to autotomize vehicles, but it doesn't feel right to the average person. It's not normal. It feels wrong.

The same is true with no longer being certain of one's death. It doesn't feel natural or right. Life sucks, why would I want to live that much longer? Or the urgency of mortality is what makes us human! These are all over-simplified platitudes. Life sucking can be heavily improved with science and a reworking of society and power structures. To be honest, if this was the world I was going to spend my eternity in, I would not want to live in it either. If anything, knowing I could live for thousands of years more forces me to try to improve the world because unlike past generations who appeared to treat life as cheap and disposable and the planet as a loaner they could junk because they wouldn't have to deal with consequences, life is even more precious and irreplaceable as is the Earth we live on and its environment. I will always have to deal with the consequences of what we do to the planet.

That said, our current religions are all religions of death. They fail to even fathom the ideas of immortality and the mindsets and applied philosophies one would need to have to deal with the knowledge that death is a choice and they could live for centuries to millennia more.

The mind would have issues dealing with it and considering how much we change in a year or a decade or a lifetime, we would become such different people that we wouldn't even recognize ourselves 1000, 2000, or a million years in the future. We would be aliens and strangers to each other. This creates vertigo as the brain didn't evolve to even process this concept.

Letting go of certainty and a concrete idea of self will have to be something to overcome. Growing up, the idea of "being yourself" out in rural Indiana was incredibly important to the point that the idea of trying to change yourself and fix a flaw was viewed almost as a sacrilegious sin. Being "who I am" means never changing, even though that is impossible. We change, we grow, and if we don't, we remain immature and self-destructive, dragging others down with us with emotion-based platitudes..

While it may not feel like it, because we are constantly flooded by 24-hour worldwide news, this is the most peaceful and most healthy time to live in the entire history of agrarian humans. Wars and poverty per person are on the decline, birth rates are dropping, because the best way to lower the population is to ensure the children can live to adulthood so the parents focus on quality of children vs quantity. 100 years ago, the average lifespan was half of what it was today, not necessarily because people died younger though people couldn't survive to be as old as our elderly can without medicine, most of it was high child and infant mortality. 2/5ths of all your children were probably not going to make it to adulthood, so you didn't become too emotionally attached to them, especially until they got past their childhood diseases. It was a hard, cruel time. My grandparents and great grandparents couldn't afford to be as close emotionally as my generation is now, and my parents' generation were just trying to drag themselves out of what was essentially abuse that was just normal for generations. PTSD from war in men was normal, causing spousal and child abuse, which lowered IQ. We pumped out heavy metals creating the most violent and now prematurely mentally aging generation in the history of the world(Schwartz, 2000).

Now China, India and Nigeria are doing the same on levels western pollution detection instruments were never designed to test for, and it scares me how war-like they may end up being in 50 years with all the pollution and poison they got hit with as kids.

For the first time in a long, long, long time, the gamble for civilization and abandoning hunter/gatherer societies is finally paying off. Life is much more precious; bonds and emotions are much more powerful and free than ever before. Humanity is just now finally reaching its true potential, connected to each other like a mind, and we have the power and time and resources to spend perfecting and improving our minds and ourselves, instead of slaving away in a factory or in the fields as mindless labor, just a famine or factory accident away from death. As someone who spent all of his life stumbling and grasping at some form and semblance of sanity and stability and understanding, I feel more like I've just been born, much like this collective conscious mind that has just been born, and science is moving at a breakneck exponential pace that will just accelerate if we push for it. I want to see what is over the horizon.

I am saying this as one in this world as a lower middle class person in the nation with the highest GDP on the planet, so I don't expect everyone to share my ideals, but life extension and eternal health are just more choices. It is neither good nor bad, it's

A Vase depicting the 8 Immortals

just now you can decide if you want to live or die.

But how do we move forward toward this possibly never-ending life? Will we be trapped being alive? I don't believe so. It's just a choice. Possible laws to get life extension may be that one will need to upgrade their education for free every decade or two, and cannot reproduce until the natural accident rate drops the population to a sustainable level, technology increases sustainability or we terraform a planet where new life can be born. If you don't want to maintain these three rules, you can easily opt out of life extension and die naturally not because you had to but because that was your choice, you

241

drove your autonomous car to work not because you had to but because you wanted to. That's what science gives you, more choice, but it makes things more complicated that way and people hate complicated things.

And that is where a new applied philosophy is needed. What I would call Immortalism. Instead of a religion or a philosophy that helps us deal with death, it would be a philosophy that helps us deal with life. Life that we don't bank on dying when it's all over, life that we have to improve and perfect because we have to live with ourselves and our planet for perhaps thousands to even millions of years, so we want it to be the best possible life.

Will we need religion? Religion such as a belief in the supernatural would probably be a big no.

Rituals, traditions and aesthetics, yes, it's a form of community and so long as it doesn't become dogmatic, it can create that sense of being part of something bigger than one's self, which is something the human mind craves thanks to our tribal based hunter/gatherer ancestors. As an applied philosophy I'd once again say, secular Buddhism is a tool in the toolbox of life. It is useful to help one decide what they should desire and be aware that desire causes suffering and eliminating that desire will reduce one's own suffering. After that the desire will be saved for empathy toward others through secular humanism.

Controlling that empathy can be part of the job of Taoism, learning when you are wasting your empathy on people who have no desire to be helped. When it comes to Buddhism's relation with death perhaps as life extension continues it will take a back seat to secular humanism and Taoism, as the Taoist religion believed in the idea that one could attain immortality and hypothesized about the philosophy of immortals.

But Buddhism's focus on helping one eliminate their own selfish desire-based suffering will be even more essential to direct that suffering into empathy. Secular humanism will tell them how to channel that empathy and Taoism will help them control that empathy and decide when the empathy is unwarranted. Taoism allows one to observe, and watch the flow of events with curiosity, not wishing to interfere, and if you do, doing it the smartest way possible.

Secular humanism will push you to want to interfere when you see injustice and slowly move us forward. It will be a balancing act, sometimes pushing forward, sometimes stepping back, sometimes withdrawing from society and conflict, sometimes charging into battle against injustice, it will require not burning out but not backing down when it really matters. I used to refer to this philosophy as Elvish Paganism based on Tolkien's elves, which already has books on the subject, not for the immortal aspects of it but for the spiritual aspects of it, much like Jediism. One of the things that always struck me about Samwise's Gamgee's

observation of elves is that one minute they could be merry and vulnerable as children and the next minute when the time required, they could be somber and serious as wise old men.

I think that may be part of the trick to dealing with living forever, breaking down our social constructs of "adulthood" and "gender", allowing our tired adult selves to have time to enjoy being kids again that society and reality of the tech at the time pushed us to abandon. To learn to be vulnerable, but also cunning, to be playful but also serious. To embrace nonsense like The Chan School or Master Chuang-tzi, to eliminate the fragmenting of our genders that we had to deny because society told us that part of ourselves is bad because you can be either one or the other and that you have the wrong genitals for embracing those emotions and traits and joys, making us half a person. Never whole. It is this duality that we will need to cultivate in ourselves, with these 3 partial and ever evolving applied philosophies.

Applied philosophies will always be essential to help one live their life and so long as they realize that applied philosophies are all lacking in some areas of life and one can hybridize them to help pick up the slack, secular Buddhism will probably always have a place in our society, moving it forward toward the better. We will have to always view self-improvement like enlightenment, like

243

overcoming biases, like world improvement, and like healing as a never-ending journey, but one worth taking. In the end, if time and the world allow us, we too may be able to call ourselves a Skeptical Buddha and one with the Scientific Tao. And that idea of what is possible fills me with so much Yugen it makes me want to try every day to move forward to that idea.

In Loving memory of
Runer, Frodhi and Melain

For more of
Eikthyrnir, Nessa and Bragnir
Follow them @two_norse_cats_and_a_fairy

Sources

Books
Ciccarelli, Saundra and Gleen E. Meyer. Psychology: My Psychlab edition. Pearson Education Inc, 2006

Coates, John. The Hour Between Dog and Wolf: Risk-taking, Gut Feelings and the Biology of Boom and Bust. Fourth Estate, 2012

Conze, Edward. Buddhist Wisdom Books: The Diamond Sutra, The Heart Sutra. Harper Torchbook, 1972

Dale, Ralph Alan. Tao Te Ching by Lao Tzu. Barnes and Noble, Inc, 2002

Davidson, Ronald M. Indian Esoteric Buddhism: A Social History of the Tantric Movement. Columbia University Press, 2002

Damasio, Antonio. Descartes' Error: Emotion, Reason, and the Human Brain. Penguin Books, 2005

Diamond, Jared. Why Sex is fun? Basic books, 1997

Graham, A.C.. The Book of Lieh tzu: A Classic of Tao. Columbia University Press Morningside Edition, 1990

Hale, Gill and Mark Evans. Feng Shui: Mind & Body, Spirit and Home. Anness Publishing Ltd. 2004

Hallowell, Edward & John Ratey. Driven to Distraction: Recognizing and Coping with Attention Deficit Disorder. Anchor; Revised edition. 2011

Harvey, P and Phra Brahmapundit. Common Buddhist Text: Guidance and Insight from the Buddha. Mahachulalongkornrajavidyalaya University Press, 2015

Ho, Kwok Man and Joanne O'Brien. The Eight Immortals of Taoism. First Meridian Printing, 1991

Hoff, Benjamin. The Tao of Pooh and the Te of Piglet. Egmont UK Ltd, 2019
Hope, Jane and Borin van Loon. Introducing Buddhism. Icon Books Ltd, 1999
Hume, N. G.. Japanese aesthetics and culture: A reader. University of New York Press.1995
Kelly, Kevin. What Technology Wants. Penguin Books, 2010
Kitagawa, Joseph. The Religious Traditions of Asia : Religion, History, and Culture. 2nd Edition, Routledge, 2002

Lakoff, George. Don't Think of an Elephant. Chelsea Green Publishing, 2004 Lorius, Cassandra. Tantric Sex: Making Love Last. Thorsons, 1999
Lynn, Steven Jay et al. Handbook of Clinical Hypnosis. Second Edition. American Psychological Association, 2010

Needham, Joseph, Ling Wang, Science and Civilisation in China, Volume 2, History of Scientific Thought, Cambridge University Press, 1956

Powers, John. Introduction to Tibetan Buddhism. Revised Edition, Snow Lion, 2007

Ray, Reginald. Indestructible Truth: The Living Spirituality of Tibetan Buddhism, Shambhala, 2002

Ronson, Jon. The Psychopath Test: A Journey Through the Madness Industry. Riverhead Books. 2011

Sutherland, Diane and Jon Sutherland, Endless Path: Buddhism. Flame Tree Publishing, 2006
Tribe, Anthony J et al. Buddhist Thought: A Complete Introduction to the Indian Tradition. Routledge, 2000

Walters, Derek. The Secrets of Chinese Astrology. Octopus Publishing Group Ltd, 2003 Watson, Burton. The Complete Works of Zhuangzi. Columbia University Press, 2013
Williams, Mark And Danny Penman. Mindfulness: An Eight-Week Plan for Finding Peace in a Frantic World. Rodale, 2011

News Articles
Baklitskaya, Kate. Mummified monk is 'not dead' and in rare meditative state, says expert. The Siberian Times. 02 February 2015
http://siberiantimes.com/other/others/news/n0105-mummified-monk-is-not-dead-and-in-rare-meditative-state-says-expert/

Levinovitz, Alan. Chairman Mao Invented Traditional Chinese Medicine. Slate. October 22, 2013

Solman Paul, Why Those Who Feel They Have Less Give More. PBS. Jun 21, 2013
https://www.pbs.org/newshour/economy/why-those-who-feel-they-have-less-give-more

Wiles, Siouxsie. Periods: The painful side of sexism lacks research and funding. Stuff Magazine. Mar 04 2019 https://www.stuff.co.nz/opinion/110957629/periods-the-painful-side-of-sexism

Journals and Magazines
Beecher, Henry. Requests for morphine by soldiers verses civilians. Journal of American Medical Association 161, 1956, p.17

Chen, Thomas and Peter Chen. The death of Buddha: a medical enquiry. J Med Biogr, 13(2) 2005 May, pp. 100-103. https://www.ncbi.nlm.nih.gov/pubmed/19813312

Cooper, Katelyn et al. Who perceives they are smarter? Exploring the influence of student characteristics on student academic self-concept in physiology. Adv Physiol Educ 42: 2018. pp. 200–208, doi:10.1152/advan.00085.2017.
https://journals.physiology.org/doi/full/10.1152/advan.00085.2017
De Dreu, Carston, et al. Oxytocin promotes Human Ethnocentrism. PNAS, 108 (4), January 25, 2011. pp. 1262-1266
https://doi.org/10.1073/pnas.1015316108

Epley, Nicholas, et al. Believers' estimates of God's beliefs are more egocentric than estimates of other people's beliefs. PNAS, 106 (51), December 22, 2009 pp. 21533-21538 https://doi.org/10.1073/pnas.0908374106

Henkel, Linda. Point-and-Shoot Memories: The Influence of Taking Photos on Memory for a Museum Tour. Psychological science Volume: 25 issue: 2, December 5, 2013, pp. 396-402 https://doi.org/10.1177/0956797613504438

Horgan, J, Why I Don't Dig Buddhism. Scientific American, December 2, 2011 https://blogs.scientificamerican.com/cross-check/why-i-dont-dig-buddhism/?fb-clid=IwAR0SDF3T58UWYm7UCt3BdBcSkCM2K5tE1Zr7xwEeyPO-RhKIb5xEULtlNPo

Kapogiannis, D, et al. Cognitive and neural foundations of religious belief, PNAS. March 9, 2009; https://www.pnas.org/content/early/2009/03/06/0811717106.abstract

Kemp, David & Kathleen Franco, Possible leukopenia associated with long-term use of echinacea. The Journal of the American Board of Family Practice / American Board of Family Practice 15(5): September 2002. pp.417-9

Kruger, J & D. Dunning. Unskilled and unaware of it: How difficulties in recognizing one's own incompetence lead to inflated self-assessments. Journal of Personality and Social Psychology, 77(6), 1999. pp. 1121–1134 https://doi.org/10.1037/0022-3514.77.6.1121

Lee, Richard B, Eating Christmas in the Kalahari, American Museum of Natural History, Dec 1969.

Mikel, Jr, Offerings to a Stone Snake Provide the Earliest Evidence of Religion, Scientific american, 2006 https://www.scientificamerican.com/article/offerings-to-a-stone-snak/

Mocan, Naci & Han Yu, Can Superstition Create a Self-Fulfilling Prophecy? School Outcomes of Dragon Children of China. National Bureau of Economic Research. Working Paper 23709 August 2017. DOI 10.3386/w23709 https://www.nber.org/papers/w23709

Neisser, U., & Harsch, N. Phantom flashbulbs: False recollections of hearing the news about Challenger. In E. Winograd & U. Neisser (Eds.), Affect and accuracy in recall: Studies of "flashbulb" memories. 1992. pp. 9–31

Nishio, Yoshiyuki. Delusions of death in a patient with right hemisphere infarction, Cogn Behav Neurol. 25(4): 2012 Dec, pp. 216-23.

Pecnerova et al. Genome-Based Sexing Provides Clues about Behavior and Social Structure in the Woolly Mammoth. Current Biology, 2017 DOI: 10.1016/j.cub.2017.09.064

Ross, Lee et al. Perseverance in Self-Perception and Social Perception: Biased Attributional Processes in the Debriefing Paradigm. Journal of Personality and Social Psychology 32(5):880-92 DOI:10.1037/0022-3514.32.5.880

Sanderson, Alex. The Śaiva Age: The Rise and Dominance of Śaivism during the Early Medieval Period. In: Genesis and Development of Tantrism. Institute of Oriental Culture, University of Tokyo, 23, 2009. pp. 41-350.

Schultz, W, et al. A computational and neural model of momentary subjective well-being. PNAS, August 4, 2014; https://doi.org/10.1073/pnas.1407535111

Schwartz, Brian et al. Past adult lead exposure is associated with longitudinal decline in cognitive function. Neurology 55(8): November 2000. pp. 1144-50

Skolnick, Alexander, & Vivian Dzokoto. Disgust and contamination: a cross-national comparison of Ghana and the United States. Psychol., 27 February 2013 https://doi.org/10.3389/fpsyg.2013.00091

Smith, M. et al. Sexually Transmitted Infection Knowledge among Older Adults: Psychometrics and Test–Retest Reliability. 17(7). April 2020. p. 2462
Staal, Fritz, Mantras and Bird Songs, Journal of the American Oriental Society 105(3). July 1985 p.549
https://www.researchgate.net/publication/272586615_Mantras_and_Bird_Songs

Thomas, JG . The early parenting of twins. Military Medicine. 161 (4): April 1996, pp. 233–235. doi:10.1093/milmed/161.4.233

Webster, D. M., & A W Kruglanski, Individual differences in need for cognitive closure. Journal of Personality and Social Psychology, 67(6), 1994. pp.1049–1062.

Wilson, Timothy D.. Just Think: The Challenges of a Disengaged mind. Science, Vol. 345, Issue 6192, 2014, pp. 75-77
https://science.sciencemag.org/content/345/6192/75

Zabelina, D. L., & Robinson, M. D.. Child's play: Facilitating the originality of creative output by a priming manipulation. Psychology of Aesthetics, Creativity, and the Arts, 4(1), 2010. pp. 57–65. https://doi.org/10.1037/a0015644

Websites
Thakur, Pallavi, How did Lord Buddha die? Speakingtree.in, 2017, https://www.speakingtree.in/allslides/how-did-lord-buddha-die

For extra in depth details on the history of Indian, China, Buddhism, Tantra, cognitive biases and Taoism
https://en.wikipedia.org/, n,d

Photo attribution

60

"Buddha" by LadyPutz

61

"Come on where are the women!" by archer10 (Dennis)

62

"The Hope Diamond" by dbking

"Lotus" by Marufish

63

Carl Sagan, from image of the Planetary Society, cropped to size

64

"Detective Bragnir" by Serra Zander

65

"Cliche stock photo o' floating teal 'n' orange math equations" by TORLEY

67

Monk" by Jamiecat

68

"Buddha" by fra-NCIS

70

"006 Sariputta" by Anandajoti

71

"Balanced on Water" by aeu04117

72

Botanical Garden, København K, Denmark

75

"China-8090 - Jade Buddha" by archer10 (Dennis)

75

"Night-time candle-lit ceremony at Wat Phan Tao on Visakha Bucha Day 2014 26" by John Shedrick

77

This East Javanese relief depicts the Buddha in his final days, and Ānanda, his chief attendant.by Anandajoti Bhikkhu

80

"Pha That Luang Shrine" by joaquinuy

81

UNESCO/A Lezine The taller Buddha of Bamiyan before (left picture) and after destruction (right). To distinguish the two statues (55 m and 37 m) from each other: Look at the form of the statues niche. The niche of the taller Buddha is much more precise

83

"Jade Buddha Temple" by lyng883

84

"Costa Rican Zen Garden" by Clearly Ambiguous

85

"The moon through a crumbling window" in the "A Hundred Aspects of the Moon" series. Bodhidharma, by Yoshitoshi, 1887

86

"Another private area in the Tenryu-ji Zen temple grounds" by shankar s.

87

Yuzen, a buddhist monk from the Sōtō Zen sect begging at Oigawa, by Arashiyama

88

"DSC21812, Byodoin Temple, Uji City, Japan" by jimg944

90

"Vishwanath Temple" by solarisgirl

91

Skull cup (Kapala) by mountain

90

"Shiva and Shakti" by Cornelia Kopp

93

Popular print of the goddess Kali, published by the Calcutta Art Studio. Lithograph, Kolkata, Bengal, India, c. 1885–1895.

94

Vajradhara Part of the tantric art exhibit Honored Father-Honored Mother, Trammell & Margaret Crow Collection of Asian Art, Dallas, Texas, USA.

95

Tripura Sundari on Pancha Brahma Asana

96

Yab-Yum, which represents the primordial union of wisdom and compassion. The male figure is usually linked to karunā, compassion, and upaya, skillful means, while the female partner relates to prajñā, insight.

97

Heruka in Yab-Yum form. On display at Gangaramaya Temple museum.

98

"Sri Yantra (Hindu)" by Tomoaki INABA

99

"Elephant smiling" by solarisgirl

100

Sharaha British Museum.jpg" by Zippymarmalade is licensed under CC BY-SA 3.0 https://creativecommons.org/licenses/by-sa/3.0/

101

Close-up of Saraha and female teacher/consort in a 19th Century Thangka. - Public Domain

103

"Female Archer, Berlin, August 2015" by leonyaakov

104

"Georg Pauli (1855-1935) - Midsummer's Night (c.1893)" by ketrin1407

106

Kushan sculpture of a yaksinī (2nd century), Mathura region

107

Sixty-four Yoginis encircle the interior walls of a 10th-century temple in Hirapur, Odisha, Eastern

108

https://www.scienceandnonduality.com/article/what-is-tantra-1

109

"His Holiness Jigdal Dagchen Sakya draws a line with a vajra into the Hevajra sand mandala closing the glowing deity palace, on a circular table, monks and students attending, Sakya Lamdre, Tharlam Monastery of Tibetan Buddhism, Boudha, Kathmandu, Nepal" by Wonderlane

110

A Vajra and a Ghanta (Bell), which are classic ritual tools and symbols of Vajrayāna Jean-Pierre Dalbéra from Paris, France - Ghanta et Vajra (British Museum)

111

"File:12th-century Kama Artha Dharma Moksha relief at Shaivism Hindu temple Hoysaleswara arts Halebidu Karnataka India 3.jpg" by Ms Sarah Welch is licensed under CC BY-SA 4.0
https://creativecommons.org/licenses/by-sa/4.0/

113

Misty Mountains by Billy tyne

115

Meditative statue with flowers Chris Ensey https://unsplash.com/@censey

116
"Eikthyrnir" by Akire Bubar
117
https://unsplash.com/@emilie_lmt
119
https://unsplash.com/@moigonz
121
"Zen Garden, Buddha" by aflavell
122
"Nessa" by Serra Zander
123
Leaf in the water by https://unsplash.com/@kellysikkema
124
"Mindfulness" by darraghoconnor12
126
"Buddha Quote 66" by h.koppdelaney
127
"1 of 6 Devas offering a gift of fruit to the Tian Tan Buddha. #taoism #buddha #buddhism #hongkong #lantauisland #china" by almccarley
128
"Buddha Quote 36" by h.koppdelaney
131
"Tranquil Japanese Garden by Freidin Design and Construction" by Landscape Design Advisor
132
"Ananda Thera, Standing Buddha, Polonnaruwa, Sri Lanka"
133
xhttps://unsplash.com/@hiro7jp removed buddha statue
134
"Laozi" by edenpictures
136
Chinese character for the word Tao by Nyo-commonswiki
139
Ritual of Taoism" by nekotank
141
View from the bamboo-boat" by magical-world
143
https://unsplash.com/@hiro7jp
144
"Taoism Temple, Aljunied, Singapore" by cattan2011
146
Confucius, Philosopher of the Chinese, published by Jesuit missionaries at Paris in 1687
147
Fourteenth of The Twenty-four Filial Exemplars by digar
148
"Melain" by Adam Collier
149
Philosopher [Mo-tzu] by Vjacheslav Rublevskiy
151
Statue of Shang Yang, an Ancient Chinese celebrity by Fanghong
152
A modern marble statue of the first Emperor of China, Qin Shi Huang by JesseW900 CC BY-SA 4.0 https://creativecommons.org/licenses/by-sa/4.0/

193

Porcelain figure of Zhongli Quan decorated in underglaze cobalt blue, Wanli period (1573-1620), Ming dynasty, Hallwyl Museum, Sweden

194

"Figure of Daoist Immortal He Xiangu" is marked with CC0 1.0

195

A woodcut of Zhang Guo, carrying a fish-drum is marked with CC0 1.0

196

"Daoist Immortal Han Xiangzi" is marked with CC0 1.0

197

"Figure of Lu Dongbin, Jingdezhen, Qing - Public Domain

198

"Chinese Figure of Lan Caihe, Qing Dynasty, Daoguang Period, 1821-1850, jadeite - Huntington Museum of Art - DSC05256.JPG" by Daderot

199

"Vase avec les huit Immortels (Shanghai Museum, Chine)" by dalbera

200

"Ivory statue of Daoist Immortal Li Tieguai a lame beggar Field Museum.jpg" by Mary Harrsch is licensed under CC BY-SA 4.0

201

The Eight Immortals crossing the sea, from Myths and Legends of China by Werner, E. T. C. (1922)

202

Zhang Lu's painting of Liezi, early 16th century - Public Domain

204

"Laojun Mtns. (in explore)" by Rod Waddington

206

"Confucious 01" by shayhaas

208

"God of Taoism" by nekotank

209

"Tranquil" by Gemma Stiles

210

Taoism, Singapore" by cattan2011

211

The eight trigrams of the I Ching, known as bagua by Benoît Stella alias BenduKiwi

212

"The Chinese Zodiac In Haw Par Villa" by lemonfilmblog

213

The carvings with Chinese Zodiac on the ceiling of the gate to Kushida Shrine in Fukuoka (mirrored image) by Jakub Hałun CC BY-SA 4.0

214

"Feng Shui master's Luopan" by wZa HK

216

Old Chinese medical chart of acupuncture meridians - public domain

217

"Accupuncture" by Lars Plougmann

219

"Feng Shui Desain Interior Warna Cat Rumah yang Cocok dengan Fengshui" by Gambar Rumah + Desain Interior ANNAHAPE GALLERY

220

"Yokohama Chinese Medicine Shark fin large.jpg" is licensed under CC BY-SA 3.0

221

Silver Falls, Mount Rainier National Park by joe parks

Made in the USA
Coppell, TX
07 May 2022

77504293R00142